ENTHRONEMENT
The Recognition of the Reincarnate Masters of Tibet and the Himalayas

ENTHRONEMENT
The Recognition of the Reincarnate Masters of Tibet and the Himalayas

by

Jamgon Kongtrul Lodrö Tayé

translated and introduced by

Ngawang Zangpo

Snow Lion Publications
Ithaca, New York

Snow Lion Publications
P.O. Box 6483
Ithaca, New York 14851 USA
Tel: 607-273-8519

Cover photo: The enthronement of the 17th Karmapa. This picture, taken on September 27, 1992, at Tsurpu Monastery, Tibet provides the mirror image of the enthronement described in this book. Here the 12th Tai Situpa officiates at the enthronement of Karmapa; this book was written for the enthronement of the 10th Tai Situpa by the 14th Karmapa. Photo by Bryan Miller.

ISBN 1-55939-083-2

Printed in Canada on recycled paper.

Library of Congress Cataloging-in-Publication Data

Koṅ-sprul Blo-gros-mtha'-yas, 1813-1899.
    [Byam mgon mchog gi sprul pa'i sku seṅ ge'i khrir phebs pa'i mandala rgyas bshad ño tshar sgo brgya 'byed pa'i dga' ston. English]
    Enthronement : the recognition of the reincarnate masters of Tibet and the Himalayas / Jamgon Kongtrul Lodrö Tayé ; translated and introduced by Ngawang Zangpo.
        p.   cm.
    Includes bibliographical references.
    ISBN 1-55939-083-2
    1. Lamas. 2. Reincarnation (Buddhism) 3. Buddhism--China--Tibet. I. Ngawang Zangpo, 1954-　. II. Title.
BQ7744.K6713 1997
294.3'4237--dc21　　　　　　　　　　　　　　　　　　　97-13259
　　　　　　　　　　　　　　　　　　　　　　　　　　　　CIP

Table of Contents

PART TWO: THE ENTHRONEMENT OF A REINCARNATE MASTER

To His Holiness the Dalai Lama,
Tai Situpa,
and Chadral Rinpoché —
the three wise men
who recognized the reincarnation
of my teacher, Kalu Rinpoché

Preface

This book began as an attempt to come to terms with an unusual event in my life: in 1991, the Dalai Lama announced that a child that I have known practically since his birth is the reincarnation of Kalu Rinpoché, the Tibetan meditation teacher and spiritual guide I had studied with from 1972 until his death in 1989. The announcement of his rebirth was good news, joyous news, incredible and wonderful news...but it signaled to me that the time had come to learn more about an aspect of Himalayan tantric Buddhism I had casually ignored — the rebirth of meditation masters who reassume their work — study, meditation, and teaching — and their thrones.

To understand the arrival in my world of a one-and-a-half-year-old "little buddha" in diapers, who was about to inherit the place once occupied by the eighty-four-year-old man I had known and loved, I turned to the writings of Jamgon Kongtrul, a meditation master of the nineteenth century. His work, always reliable and authoritative, provided the authentic picture I was searching for. It offers a traditional view of the enthronement of reincarnate masters, with not the slightest attempt at interpretation for a modern audience.

I was unable to find any book by Jamgon Kongtrul on the related subject of how such children are recognized as reincarnate masters: I doubt that he wrote such a book or that one exists by any Tibetan writer. To answer some of my questions on that subject, I visited Tai Situpa, a Tibetan meditation master who is often asked by Tibetans of all schools to find reincarnate masters. He is not the only modern master who does this work, but I chose to interview him for two reasons. First, the present-day Tai Situpa is, in the eyes of Tibetan Buddhists, the same person that we read of in Kongtrul's book. Kongtrul eagerly awaited the enthronement of the reincarnation of his teacher, the tenth Tai Situpa; the Tai Situpa who speaks of his work as a finder of reincarnate masters in the interview is the twelfth of the line. Second, as is mentioned in the course of the interview, Tai Situpa was the master responsible for first suggesting to the Dalai Lama the identity of my teacher's reincarnation. This is a connection that is significant to me personally, and I feel deeply grateful for that act.

Thus, *Enthronement* focuses on two aspects of the life of reincarnate lamas: their recognition and their enthronement. In making this text available in English, I hope it will contribute to an accurate picture of this crucial aspect of the spiritual life of the Himalayan region as it was and as it continues to be. While I have wished to be as objective as possible in presenting this information, I cannot pretend to be impartial toward the reincarnate masters of Tibet. Since I began studying under the guidance of Tibetan meditation masters in 1972, I have met close to one hundred men and one woman (the remarkable Khandro Rinpoché) who are acknowledged as reincarnate masters. Whether one chooses to believe in reincarnation or dismisses the idea as nonsense, I believe anyone would be struck by these individuals. If the outstanding qualities they seem to share — uncommon compassion, patience, vigor, wisdom, humor, loving-kindness, goodness, and often genius — are due to a selection system capable of recognizing prodigies before they are able to talk, it is a system that deserves serious study. If these impressive individuals are the results of education and environment alone, these are equally commendable; extraordinary, in fact, and probably unique. The goal of Buddha's teaching and of Himalayan Buddhist culture is to produce not Buddhists but buddhas, enlightened persons. It is this goal of enlightenment that I feel Tibet's great masters personify and it is with the wish that their wisdom be added to the sum of enlightenment in the world that this book is written.

Acknowledgments

At the end of writing this book, I am very happy to look back and thank once again the persons who helped me with this project.

The heart of *Enthronement* lies in the words of Jamgon Kongtrul that I have tried to render in readable English. I would like to assure you that I have managed to capture both the substance and the style of his every word and meaning, but I cannot make such claims. Some errors in content have undoubtedly escaped my notice despite the invaluable, generous help offered me by the Tibetan lamas, reincarnate and ordinary, whose names are listed here. First and foremost is Tai Situ Rinpoché: quite simply, I would not have done this translation without his permission. In fact, I asked for and was refused that permission in 1989, soon after the death of Kalu Rinpoché. To my second request, some years later, he assented and gave me his indispensable support — the interview transcribed in this book, replies to questions on certain difficult passages in the book, and assurance of the cooperation of his two constant lama-companions who are known to anyone who has met Tai Situpa: Gégen (his elderly teacher) and Shastri (his personal secretary). Both lamas helped by finding the time to answer many questions concerning the original text. Similarly, I feel blessed to have had the full cooperation of Tsa-tsa Drubgen Rinpoché, a senior Kagyu *tulku* who lives in the town, Dartsendo (or Kanding), that marks the border between Kham (East Tibet) and Sichuan province, China. Lastly, Tulku Thubten, a young reincarnate master from Amdo (East Tibet) who now lives in California, has lived up to his title of "Rinpoché" (precious one): he is not yet thirty years old but exudes the brilliance, depth, and experience that one would expect in a much more mature teacher.

At different stages of this translation, I have been the guest of a number of close friends whose material support has allowed me to continue my work on this book. My heartfelt thanks go to Lama Gyaltsen of Sonada Monastery, Faye Angevine and Howard Brewer of Taipei, Koji Hirota and his family of Tokyo, and, most particularly, Kathleen Bryan and Richard Melton of Kailua, Hawaii. Along the way, I have been helped in this translation work in significant ways by these dear friends: Jane Perkins, Leslie Robinson (Lama Tsering), Margy Hamai, Tamiko Onodera, and my wife, Marie-Laure Jacquet (Naljorma Tenma).

Finally, I am very touched by the support and encouragement I have received from Jeffrey Cox, Sidney Piburn, Susan Kyser, and Kate Bloodgood, who contribute greatly to our wealth of Buddhist literature under the banner of Snow Lion Publications.

Introduction

Enthronement presents a subject that is deeply rooted in the lives of the Buddhist peoples of the Himalayas: the rebirth and enthronement of their spiritual leaders. Even the most casual contact with the culture, politics, or religion of Tibet and the surrounding region brings outsiders face-to-face with reincarnate lamas. Although every form of Buddhism makes reincarnation a cornerstone of its doctrine and many recognize that some of their greatest spiritual masters exhibit a strong propensity for spiritual life from early childhood, the recognition and enthronement of reincarnate masters is unique to Himalayan tantric Buddhism. To Tibetans and to others in the Himalayan region who share their faith, the reappearance of past masters seems as natural as sunrise: the sun which shone yesterday will rise again today; the master whose life once lit the world will reappear among us. While some might ask why the Tibetans alone acknowledge the reincarnations of their spiritual leaders, a Tibetan would wonder why other Buddhist cultures do not: the recognition and enthronement of reincarnate masters have provided the principal source of spiritual renewal for Himalayan Buddhists for the last thousand years. This tradition is both uniquely Tibetan and genuinely Buddhist.

This *Introduction* locates the subject of reincarnate meditation masters within its two major contexts — in the activity of bodhisattvas, a concept at the core of Buddhism; and in modern Tibetan society. To help bring these subjects from the realm of the abstract to real life, I have also included an account of my experience of the death and rebirth of one reincarnate master — my teacher, Kalu Rinpoché.

The main text of *Enthronement* is divided into two parts: Part One contains an interview with Tai Situ Rinpoché, a reincarnate master and one of the leaders of modern Tibetan Buddhism, whose responsibilities include the recognition of other reincarnate lamas. During the course of the interview, Tai Situpa explains many aspects of his work as a modern seer whose indications have directed wise men bearing gifts and good news to homes of newborn bodhisattvas throughout the Himalayan region. Part Two contains the book at the heart of *Enthronement*, a translation of a Tibetan text written in 1859 by Jamgon Kongtrul, a meditation master who wrote for those who joined him in welcoming the arrival of the child believed to be the reincarnation of their spiritual leader. This "little buddha" was the same Tai Situpa two lifetimes ago!

The Appendix contains a list of the series of incarnations of Karmapa and Tai Situpa with their years of birth and death, plus two short texts. The first, by Kongtrul, describes the red crown which has for centuries been the trademark of Tai Situpa. The second, an extract from a book by a committee of modern Tibetan scholars, provides some details of the life of the child for whom the book translated in Part Two was written, Tai Situpa Péma Kunzang.

A HISTORICAL PERSPECTIVE

The story behind *Enthronement* — the recognition and enthronement of reincarnate meditation masters — began in 1288, the year a great Tibetan yogi, Orgyenpa (1230-1309), recognized a four-year-old boy as the reincarnation of his master, Karma

Pakshi (1204-1283). The child became renowned as the third Karmapa, whose succession of lives in Tibet began with that of a meditation master named Dusum Kyenpa (1110-1193).

This proved a momentous event in Tibetan history. The child, Karmapa Rangjung Dorjé (1284-1339), is remembered today not only as one of the greatest Karmapas but as one of Tibet's foremost meditators, visionaries, and writers. His success ushered in the age of *tulkus*, the reincarnate masters who continue to preserve, nurture, and lead Buddhist practice in the Tibetan-speaking regions of the Himalayas. All schools of Tibetan Buddhism adopted the so-called tulku system: at the death of a spiritual leader, his or her reincarnation is sought out through meditation, in visions, or in signs, and the designated child is then invited to continue his or her life's training and work in the institutions of his or her previous incarnation.

These origins of the recognition of reincarnate spiritual masters in Tibet are well known. What has been left unrecorded is whether such a custom existed in India — Orgyenpa, the yogi responsible for the first such recognition in Tibet, had traveled widely in India before meeting the child he recognized as his master reincarnate. Had he met officially designated tulkus during his travels? Only a study of his very extensive biography could possibly answer that question. The two Tibetan sources I have read that mention Orgyenpa's designation of Rangjung Dorjé as a tulku both specify that this event was the first of its kind "in Tibet," which leaves to the realm of speculation the question of whether such a system existed elsewhere.

While the antecedents of the tulku system are unclear, examples of Tibetan masters before the thirteenth century who remembered their past lives are well documented. To give some examples, Karma Pakshi, Orgyenpa's master, became known as the reincarnation of Dusum Kyenpa, but only due to his own recollection, which was provoked by events in his life at the age of fifty. Before him, the great Tibetan yogini Machik Labdron (1031-1129) recounted to her students her past life as an Indian yogi, and she claimed to have been the reincarnation of two women central to the early spread of Buddhism to Tibet, the Tibetan Yeshé Tsogyal and the Indian Sukasiddhi. Before her, the king of all Tibet's spiritual kings, the Indian yogi Padmasambhava or "Guru Rinpoché," predicted that his close Tibetan disciples would take rebirth with the power to recall their past lives and the locations of the treasure texts he concealed throughout the Himalayan region for the benefit of future generations of Buddhists. The first such treasure-revealer, Sangyé Lama, lived from about 1000 until 1080.

Thus, whether or not either formal or informal systems of recognition of reincarnate masters existed in parts of India prior to Buddhism's reaching Tibet, such a system quickly evolved in the Himalayas. A major catalyst for it was the founding of monasteries throughout the Himalayan region during the eleventh and twelfth centuries. By that time, Buddhism had become popular and had assimilated into the language and culture of Tibet: Orgyenpa, who recognized Tibet's first infant tulku, was the last Tibetan master to return from India with an entirely new (within the Tibetan world) system of meditation techniques. His life and this single act of recognition thus mark a significant turning point in Tibetan history. Tulkus were there to stay, not only as embodiments of a glorious Tibetan past but as ambassadors from the tantric motherland, India. As links between Tibet and India became tenuous, a connection between Tibet and the homeland of the Buddha was maintained by stories of the Tibetan reincarnate masters' past lives as the great masters of India. In the main text below, Kongtrul mentions a number of reincarnate masters of his circle and traces the thread of their past lives back to the Holy Land. At the very least, this reading of history lent legitimacy and an aura of tradition to what was in fact a unique innovation in the Buddhist world.

With recognition of child reincarnations and their installation at the head of Buddhist institutions came formal ceremonies of investiture, called enthronements. The child was placed on the throne of the predecessor and a ritual of acknowledgment of the infant as the successor performed. Although we might assume that the first recognition of a tulku was accompanied by an enthronement, one book that traces the lives of the leaders of the lineage of the Karmapas does not explicitly mention an enthronement until 1450, when the second Tai Situpa was enthroned by the sixth Karmapa. Among the Karmapas themselves, Chödrak Gyatso, enthroned as the seventh Karmapa at the age of nine months in 1454, is the first credited with having received that honor. (It should be mentioned that these dates were culled from only one source;[1] other histories may place the origins of this ceremony well in advance of these dates.)

This long-standing tradition of recognition and enthronement of reincarnate masters remains alive within the Tibetan-speaking Himalayan region. Most of the masters who have attracted the adoration and faith of the Tibetan people and the admiration and respect of non-Tibetans are reincarnate masters — tulkus. Almost all of these were searched out and recognized in very early childhood and then given an intense religious education. One might debate whether it is the education or the selection that produces such wonderful results, but few doubt the efficiency of the Tibetan system among those who have had the opportunity to meet such "greats" of the Tibetan galaxy of masters as the tulkus His Holiness the Dalai Lama, Sakya Trizin, Dezhung Rinpoché, Dilgo Kyentsé Rinpoché, Dujom Rinpoché, Minling Trichen, Karmapa, and Drukchen Rinpoché, to name but a very few of recent years.

BODHISATTVAS: SPIRITUAL HEROES AND HEROINES

The reincarnate lamas of the Himalayan region — Tibet, Nepal, northern India, Sikkim, and Bhutan — are ultimately not political or even religious leaders: they are what are known as *bodhisattvas* (Sanskrit; literally, "beings who have awakened"). Bodhisattvas vow to return continually to this or to any world where others have not awakened to their innate buddha-nature, the bottomless well of love, wisdom, and creative energy which is the nature of every sentient creature's mind. Much of Buddhism is centered around the training of bodhisattvas, to foster their aspirations, refine their motivation, strengthen their resolve, expand their horizons, and deepen their wisdom. They are said to be disengaged from this world due to their insightful understanding, but equally disdainful of self-absorbed states of enlightenment due to the overpowering compassion they feel toward the sufferings of others. In fact, true enlightenment is said to be impossible for anyone who has not sincerely embraced the bodhisattva's ideal.

Bodhisattvas find their home in the world, in the myriad realms of beings. If they choose to go to heaven when they die, they do so with the intention of bringing some enlightening spirit to a realm Buddhists conceive of as heedlessly happy and mindlessly self-absorbed. If bodhisattvas choose to go to hell at death, they do so to continue to live there as they lived on earth: with more concern for others' welfare than for their own. Bodhisattvas vow to use their every lifetime to help others, to be as stable and as impartially beneficial to all as the sun, the moon, the air, fire, water, or earth. However, they are not otherworldly Boy or Girl Scouts: bodhisattvas have awakened and are dedicated to helping others awaken. This is the reason for all their acts: they may bring comfort and solace to those traumatized by material or emotional loss; they may provide stimulation for the apathetic or the self-content; they may foster peaceful wisdom in the habitually active or active compassion in the wise; they may open the doors to tranquillity for those whose minds are never at rest; or they may inspire insight and creativity in those who have found a separate but sterile personal peace. But whatever bodhisattvas do to help others materially or spiritually, their deepest aspiration remains to free all living things from all forms of suffering by guiding them to the spiritual awakening of enlightenment. Until all living beings find this freedom, these heroes and heroines with a thousand faces in as many walks of life never consider themselves free.

Tibet's reincarnate masters are in fact living bodhisattvas who have dedicated their lives, lifetime after lifetime, to serving others. Specifically, these reincarnate lamas are bodhisattvas whose principal role is to ensure the continuation of the religious institutions and spiritual life of Himalayan tantric Buddhism. Among bodhisattvas, they probably amount to a small subgroup, if Buddhist theory is to be credited: bodhisattvas are said to work in countless ways to assist others in every land and culture. This need not be as Buddhists or as Buddhist spiritual leaders in Buddhist cultures (although this is the focus of reincarnate lamas' lives). A bodhisattva's vow is to help all beings, to uplift their lives materially and spiritually so they can experience the natural freedom and enlightenment of their own minds: in short, to help them become buddhas, not necessarily Buddhists.

To illustrate, the following passages provide an example of a meditation master's explanation to Tibetan readers of bodhisattvas' activities throughout the world and of their lives as reincarnate lamas in Tibet. The writer is Jamgon Kongtrul, one of the greatest masters of the nineteenth century; these quotations are taken from his *Biography of Jamyang Kyentsé Wongpo*, the life story of his teacher and friend. In this first passage he describes Kyentsé as an enlightened bodhisattva who intentionally takes rebirth throughout the world in animate and inanimate forms to help others. Although Kongtrul mentions just one individual here, these words could apply to any bodhisattva. He underlines that belief by citing passages from the Buddha's teachings:

> *The Flower Ornament Discourse* states:
>> Though awakening's ocean they've fully attained,
>> An ocean of others in darkness remain —
>> To bring beings' minds to full maturation,
>> They show an ocean of enlightened intentions
>> And continual oceans of unclouded deeds:
>> The joyful ones' manifestations are these!
>
> Since beginningless time he [Jamyang Kyentsé Wongpo] has been fully enlightened within the sphere of totality,

the body of unadulterated simplicity, the perfection of wisdom. While remaining unperturbed within this state, his great pervasive compassion directly perceives the nature of the infinite numbers of beings who have fallen prey to delusion. The innate energy of this compassion creates the designs of oceans of pure realms and forms called bodies of the perfect splendor of enlightenment. These transform themselves in appropriate response to the needs of others in an endless dance of magical play: some produce emanations to guide certain individuals to the spiritual path; others do not have one specific goal. In either case his enduring, continual cycle of activity in the past, present, and future finds him remaining within cyclic existence for many eons even for the benefit of a single being without this provoking the slightest feeling of discouragement. This manner of aiding others exceeds the limits of our imagination. *The Lamp of the Jewels Discourse* states:

> Kings among poets for whom verse is dominion;
> Dancers, and drummers, athletes, and musicians;
> Dancers who garlands of great beauty bear;
> Master magicians who show forms everywhere;
> Villagers, mayors, and the leaders of men;
> Merchants, home-owners, and guiding companions;
> Monarchs and ministers, messengers, counsel;
> Doctors whose textbooks prescribe worldly rituals;
> Forests of trees in deep wilderness groves;
> Medicine, treasures in inexhaustible troves;
> Trees of abundance, gems of wish-granting force;
> For those who are lost, the path's correct course.

As stated here, his emanations of enlightenment provide others with either temporary or lasting comfort and happiness. In the vast expanse of universes in the ten directions simultaneously, his supreme physical manifestations of enlightenment display the twelve acts of the Buddha. His manifestations also appear as ordinary beings: as bodhisattvas, followers of Buddha, solitary sages, erudite scholars, accomplished awareness-holders, persons practicing virtue, universal monarchs, lesser rulers, government ministers, priests, householders, birds, deer, etc. They can manifest as created forms which help others, such as the

creations of the eighteen kinds of craft; or in inanimate
form, such as wish-fulfilling jewels, medicine, food, clothes,
mountains, trees, boats, bridges, etc. *The Extensive Tantra
of Great Illusion* states:

> In worlds in ten directions' space,
> On each and every atom,
> Great compassion's blessings' trace —
> Buddha's acts no mind can fathom.
> Though no one can ever find
> The far bounds of beings he leads,
> Through his body, speech, and mind,
> Talents, spontaneous activity.
> Beings' wretched realms he transforms as pure,
> For them, full awakening's made real,
> And completed cultivation sure
> Of wisdom everywhere revealed. (3a-4a)

Kongtrul has ended this passage with a list of the four ways
enlightenment physically manifests in this world:[2] in its supreme form — a historical Buddha who performs the twelve
acts of a Buddha; as an ordinary being; as a piece of art — this
includes painting, sculpture, music, dance; and as an inanimate
form. These are all called *tulku* in Tibetan. The men and women
who have been recognized and enthroned as reincarnate masters fall into the second category, that of enlightenment manifest as ordinary individuals. Nonetheless, when Kongtrul in
the text below and other writers elsewhere repeatedly refer to
their preferred reincarnate masters as "supreme manifestations
of enlightenment," such language signals that the writer has
departed from the realm of scholarship to that of poetry.

The preceding passage has described the bodhisattva's acts
in general; the following passage from the same text highlights
the difference between our consciousness and way of taking
birth, and those of bodhisattvas. Kongtrul introduces us to
Jamyang Kyentsé Wongpo as an incarnate spiritual master who
had been reborn in a series of lifetimes within the system of
Himalayan tantric Buddhism. Kyentsé is credited as having
been, among many others, a reincarnation of both Gampopa

and Réchungpa, contemporaries who were the two foremost disciples of Tibet's great yogi-poet, Milarepa. Non-Tibetan readers who find this difficult to comprehend may take heart in Kongtrul's admission that this is in fact difficult for *anyone* to understand, even for Tibetans, who belong to a culture suffused with tales of great lamas, their emanations, and their return:

> Some of these emanations have appeared simultaneously, others have appeared earlier or later during the same lifetime, but most have followed one after the last. When we examine this list [of Kyentsé's past lives], it is difficult to intellectually analyze it; however, it must be said that this is not the case of an ordinary person whose consciousness takes rebirth in a series of lives throughout the three worlds driven by the force of his or her own acts, i.e., a consciousness that leaves a previous body at death and enters a new womb impelled by the creative energy of previous acts. Instead, this is a case of an individual who rests in spiritually advanced states and, by the strength of his or her aspirations and compassion, surpasses the domain of single or multiple births: the magical play of his or her innate awareness reveals itself in any form whatsoever that can serve others. He or she resembles the sun, which although just one form in the sky, will appear reflected in as many containers of water as can be placed on the ground. *The Highest Continuity* states:

> > In every pure disciple,
> > A bowl of water's clear reflection —
> > The infinite, simultaneous
> > Dawning of the Buddha's sun.

> Further, *The Ornament of the Discourses* states:

> > In many places, at one time, the Wheel is turned in
> >   myriad ways;
> > At other sites, no birth appears; in some, beings' acts
> >   make rich displays;
> > Here, complete awakening's gained; there, pain's
> >   transcendence shown —
> > Yet never from enlightenment's place is any movement
> >   ever known. (7a-7b)

To use the metaphor Kongtrul introduces here, in the case of reincarnate masters, the sun is the fully awakened state of mind of a bodhisattva; the containers of water, the groups of disciples and institutions the bodhisattva returns to guide in the form of a tulku. These public lives as institutionalized meditation masters and monastic administrators are obviously considered by Kongtrul (and by other Buddhist thinkers) to represent a small fraction of the acts performed by one individual bodhisattva.

Finally, in Buddhist theory, the whole notion of a tulku, enlightenment made physically manifest, is related to the three bodies of enlightenment. The first, the ultimate body (*dharmakaya* in Sanskrit), has no form; the language used to refer to it often employs the terms *sphere of totality, unadulterated simplicity*, or *the perfection of wisdom* (these three from the first citation translated above) and stresses its all-pervasive, formless quality. The second, the body of enlightenment's perfect splendor (*sambhogakaya* in Sanskrit), comprises the infinite multitude of forms that arise from the ultimate body's fertile ground of wisdom and compassion; the language used to refer to it often employs the terms *spontaneous, self-arising, innate energy, pure realms*, and the number five, as in *five wisdoms, five buddha-families, five colors*, and *five aspects of Buddha* — body, speech, mind, qualities, and activity. What we refer to as "meditation deities," the vast range of peaceful and wrathful deities of the Buddhist tantric pantheon, are such forms. Just as the ultimate body provides the ground for the body of perfect splendor, this in turn overflows into the myriad forms of physically manifest forms of enlightenment, "tulku" in Tibetan (*nirmanakaya* in Sanskrit). The language used to refer to this "form body" stresses its role to benefit others, its responsiveness to others' needs, and its versatility in adopting whatever form can best serve the needs of others. It should be noted that while some religions live uncomfortably with neighboring denominations which fashion entirely different beliefs and rites from the same source teachings, Buddhist theory on the subject of tulkus —

enlightenment manifest in the world — seems to anticipate this diversity and to find Buddhism's good-natured adaptability a cause for self-congratulation.

The subject of the three bodies of enlightenment is central to Buddhism and deserves far more attention than this short paragraph. However, in an effort to simplify the explanation of the three even further, one simile can be used: the ultimate, formless, all-pervasive body is like the sky — boundless and beyond the grasp of our conventional minds. The body or bodies of enlightenment's splendor emerge from this sky like clouds, reflecting the infinite variety of enlightenment's qualities in forms that lie within ordinary persons' conceptual boundaries. These clouds of enlightenment's many forms and aspects produce manifest forms of enlightenment — tulkus — which come to earth like rain, for the good of all.

THE TULKU SYSTEM IN MODERN TIBETAN SOCIETY

Although some children born to parents outside the Himalayan region have been recognized as reincarnate masters, these represent but a tiny fraction — perhaps a dozen among the thousand alive today. By and large, the system remains Himalaya-based and will probably continue to be so as long as their education facilities and the institutions these masters are reborn to serve remain viable. Some Western Buddhists debate whether and how the system could be changed or better adapted to their needs, but these masters will probably continue to be born and raised to serve the needs of the Tibetan-speaking community before any other. These men and women are regarded by the members of the Himalayan Buddhist community as their most precious treasures. Tibetans have accepted these masters as their spiritual leaders for centuries and they have complete confidence, based on their long experience, that when the sun of their teacher's life has set, a new sun of his or her rebirth will return after a short night. Tibetans discuss among themselves how to improve their system for training reincarnate masters, but their deep faith in it and the leaders it produces is never in doubt. Perhaps we could compare our attitude toward airplanes: spectacular crashes are common knowledge but few among us would propose or support an end to air travel because of those tragedies. Similarly, Tibetans are not naive: they know their system is not foolproof nor free from occasional abuse. It may not be perfect, but it is a major part of the life-blood of their culture. That having been said, two questions which modern Tibetans face concerning the reincarnate lama system can be shared with a wider readership: its inclusion of children and its exclusion of women.

Difficult Choices for Modern Tibetan Parents

It is not an ethical dilemma most parents or societies have to face: if one is reasonably sure that a child is a reincarnation of a genius in a particular field, what does one do? This is not a question of a child who shows a special aptitude for music, for example, at three or five years of age. A Tibetan child may be three or five *months* old when a meditation master informs the parents that their child was a gifted scholar, or a master meditator, or a valued spiritual leader in his or her last life. Does one wait for the child to reach maturity before allowing him or her to choose a career? If it could be proven to us that Shakespeare's (or Beethoven's, or Einstein's) reincarnation could be recognized, his or her talent nourished by a supportive environment, and that the results of such training consistently led to the greater happiness of the child and society-at-large, would we accept that system? Would we deny the world another Shakespeare, Beethoven, or Einstein? Would we prefer to leave the child in a "natural" setting — tending yaks and chickens on a farm, for example — for fear of controlling a child's life, or of stifling his or her own creativity and inclinations with our needs and ambitions? These are questions most Tibetan parents have answered by allowing the child to be enthroned in the position of his or her predecessor and to enter an education centered on religious training to the exclusion of all else.

One of the side effects of this junior lama system has been the inclusion of young children in the monasteries. Even if a boy is not deemed exceptional, many have been forced to enter a life devoted to religious training. Tibetan boys from six or seven years of age are routinely entrusted by their parents to the complete care of the monasteries: in most cases, the parents must surrender any legal hold on the child; the monastery assumes the rights and responsibilities of guardianship. Although the child is free to leave the institution at maturity, a decision at that time to divorce himself from all that he has known since early childhood must surely be traumatic. It must also be difficult to face life as a young adult if the education one has received finds no sympathetic resonance within oneself because the decision to enter a monastery was not based on an informed choice. In the old days, a childhood spent in the monastery used to be one of the only alternatives to illiteracy: no public secular school system existed in precommunist Tibet. Now, however, with public education available throughout the Himalayan region, more and more Tibetans are reconsidering this aspect of their society. While they accept that young reincarnate masters can thrive in a monastic environment from an early age, they are beginning to question the wisdom of asking average children to follow that example. The results of perpetuating that custom in the modern world — plenty of deadwood in the monasteries and many young men who leave the monasteries with only a superficial religious education behind them and few career opportunities ahead of them — have made many parents decide to send their children to secular schools.

The question of spiritual child-brides — children betrothed to a religion by their parents — should be an issue outside of traditional societies like that of the Tibetans, but it is often left unaddressed. We frown upon arranged marriages in which the only consenting adults at the altar are the parents of the bride and groom, but we think nothing of children being carried or encouraged by well-meaning parents to be baptized, saved, confirmed, given refuge, etc. Surely the decision of what faith one embraces is as important as one's choice of marriage partner and should similarly be reserved for adults only, regardless of the religious beliefs of the adults responsible for the child and regardless of the intensity of the spiritual "puppy love" ("puppy faith"?) a child or adolescent might feel.

The Tibetans once saw monasteries full of young boys — reincarnate lamas and ordinary youngsters alike — as guarantees of their culture's continuity. A new view that is becoming more prevalent maintains that young reincarnate lamas should be offered the best religious training possible from an early age but that average children should first complete their education in secular schools before they decide to spend their lives in a monastery or religious institution. To many this would guarantee the quality, if not quantity, of the members of future Himalayan Buddhist religious institutions.

The Lack of Choices for Modern Tibetan Women

In theory, the form of Buddhism practiced in northern Asia, including Tibet, accords women equal status to men. In practice, Buddhist India and Nepal of many centuries ago produced a handful of exceptional women masters and seem, with hindsight, to have been somewhat more enlightened in this domain than other Asian countries, which later grafted Buddhism onto their own cultures. A few wonderful women of wisdom appeared at the inception of Buddhism in Tibet but the eventual marriage of politics and religion in that country seems to have doomed women to minor roles. It was always possible for women to practice meditation and to attain enlightenment, but they did not expect to be admitted to most religious institutions. Organized religion was a game only men played in Tibet. Women were generally relegated to the supporting roles of cheerleaders, tea-bearers, wives of venerable masters, or mothers of their reincarnations. It didn't have to be that way, nor, more importantly, does it have to continue to be that way.

The tantric Buddhism practiced by most Tibetans maintains that women are at least the equals of men in terms of their spiritual potential. Tibetan Buddhism does not quarrel with the idea of female bodhisattvas or female buddhas (although every "historical Buddha," such as Buddha Shakyamuni, is said to be male). An example of a woman held in high regard by all Tibetan Buddhists is Niguma, a tenth-century Indian woman meditation master. She is considered to have been fully enlightened; the meditations she taught have been preserved and practiced in Tibet for centuries. One prayer of aspiration she wrote is called *The Royal Prayer of Aspirations*; a short excerpt of it provides an example of the all-embracing concerns of a bodhisattva, male or female:

> Beyond realms of beings, or oceans' far depths,
> The limits of space and totality's breadths:
> My wishes, mind's grasp, wisdom's activities
> Shall measure in every direction exceed.

> Numberless wheel-monarchs I will become —
> All peoples' hopes met by religious kingdoms;
> Ruler of every realm throughout all space,
> In perfect contentment all beings I'll place.

> When ages of weapons and sicknesses bring
> To those of the future extreme suffering,
> As supreme queen of healers I'll come, bringing peace —
> From suffering in instants I'll give sure release.

> In famines when hunger and thirst's the sole fare,
> My clouds of great wealth to sky's breadths will compare —
> Food, drink, and fine clothing; gold and silver's rich treasures —
> In all ten directions I'll rain every pleasure.

> 'Til the seas of existence all empty and dry
> By waves of awakening's good conduct, I
> For all living beings whose hosts fill the sky
> Will in ways suiting each act as spiritual guide. (2a-b)

Tibetan monks would recite this prayer, dedicate their lives to the practice of her instructions, and accept the idea of female bodhisattvas like her active throughout the world, but would ignore the fact that a woman in their culture could not share their opportunity to enjoy Niguma's inspiration in most Buddhist institutions. This is not a new story, even in Buddhism: Indian Buddhists taught the Tibetans the story of Tara, an Indian princess of yore who was so incensed at a monk's advice that she should wish to be reborn a man that she vowed to always be reborn a woman. She also vowed to single-handedly surpass the efforts of all male buddhas combined, as Niguma does in this passage from the same prayer:

> The ocean of victors of all times and directions
> Were once mundane persons, became bodhisattvas, and then
> For vast ages aspiring awakening they strived;
> Merit, wisdom complete, to enlightenment arrived.
>
> By their oceans of talents, an abundant dominion,
> They matured countless beings and led them to freedom.
> The full sum of these buddhas' aspirations and deeds
> May my own aspirations and acts far exceed! (2b)

Tara became one of the most popular bodhisattvas in the Tibetan pantheon; praises and prayers are sung to her in virtually every Tibetan monastery every morning. Yet Tara incarnate as a Tibetan woman would not have been welcome in their assemblies, their schools and colleges, and their meditation centers.

Reincarnate masters have rarely been female because the institutions most tulkus are reborn to serve are exclusively male. A few outstanding Tibetan women meditation masters have appeared over the centuries, but they seem to have been reluctant to found institutions. Whatever the reason for this, the current lack of religious institutions for women of the Himalayan region is the most urgent crisis modern Tibetan Buddhism must face. Tibetan-speaking women of the Himalayas must be admitted into existing institutions or new schools must be created to serve them and, in the traditional manner, female reincarnate masters recognized to lead them. In the past, Tibetan religious leaders could blame the female victims of exclusion from educational institutions for their sorry state: they could point to the illiterate women of the culture and claim that they were unsuited to the arduous demands of spiritual training. These days most Tibetan parents encourage their daughters' education as much as their sons'. I have met Tibetan women doctors, dentists, lawyers, journalists, engineers, administrators, bankers, zoologists, teachers, international airline hostesses, aerobics teachers, travel agents, artists, businesswomen, computer experts, and elected members of the Tibetan government. This advancement of the women of the Himalayas is the most wonderful event of the last forty turbulent years in the region. Yet if any of these women wanted to devote a few years of her life to the study or practice of Buddhism, she would probably be much better off going to the West and searching for a teacher and institutions where her gender did not disqualify her from admission. When Tibetan masters left the Himalayan region they founded equal opportunity Buddhist institutions in foreign countries, but those they call home still lag far behind.[3]

DEATH AND REBIRTH AMONG THE TIBETANS

Kalu Rinpoché (1905-1989)

When Jamgon Kongtrul died during the last days of 1899, the thousands who were touched by the event undoubtedly felt that an era had ended with his passing. However, Kongtrul had not abandoned his disciples and his work: he reincarnated not as one child but as five, each claimed by a monastery with which he had been closely related. Thus, his reincarnations are known with a prefix added to their names — usually the name of a monastery — as in Palpung Kongtrul, Zhéchen Kongtrul, etc. One, a son of the fifteenth Karmapa, became the lineage holder of the Karmapa's Oral Instruction Lineage; others were educated within other lineage's traditions. One child, born

Kalu Rinpoché (1905-1989), reincarnation of Jamgon Kongtrul Lodrö Tayé. This formal portrait was taken five months before his death. (Photo: Don Farber)

within a family descended from the first Karmapa, was recognized as Kongtrul's reincarnation, but his father, himself a reincarnate lama and disciple of Jamgon Kongtrul, refused the gifts presented to the child as well as the invitation by the monastery to have the child enthroned and installed at their institution. This child was never enthroned and was never assimilated into an institutional environment. Even the monastery he joined as a youth was relatively unique in that it was not led by a reincarnate master: the spiritual chief was chosen democratically and changed at regular intervals. The child became known to us as Kalu Rinpoché.

Because he was never enthroned, Kalu Rinpoché had no official standing, title, or recognition, but by the same token, he enjoyed perfect freedom from any responsibility to an institution. He guarded that freedom and used it to become a meditation master: he completed a three-year, three-month retreat during his late adolescence and later spent a twelve-year period wandering in isolated areas, alone or with a companion, meditating while living in tents or in caves. While it is impossible (and unwise) to try to gauge a spiritual master's level of attainment, particularly when the one in question is one's own, I think most informed, objective persons would situate Kalu Rinpoché among the great masters of this modern era.

It was Kalu Rinpoché's destiny to play a significant role in bringing Tibetan Buddhism to the attention of people the world over. He was well suited for the role of goodwill ambassador: he would remark that some people describe a glass as half empty and others, as half full, but both are correct. His natural inclination was to see the fullness in life, to always accentuate the positive similarities among people. His generous sense of humor and sense of human-ness were infallible. He never seemed to feel distant or different from anyone facing him: he was a true citizen of the world, and his innate, simple human warmth and openness were appreciated the world over.

I became a student of Kalu Rinpoché in 1972 and continued to study with him until his death in 1989. During that time I learned Tibetan and served as his translator on occasion in Europe and North America but mainly throughout Asia, particularly during the last three years of his life. Although he usually spoke his highly personal, idiosyncratic version of Lhasa Tibetan (his second language), people everywhere of all ages and backgrounds felt that he understood them and that they understood him. He had a natural facility for communication that I witnessed and marveled at, time and again. And even though Rinpoché always spoke through a translator, I should add that his ability to touch people's hearts had little to do with his translators. When he spoke through his best translator-students — Richard Barron (Lama Chökyi Nyima) in English, or François Jacquemart (Lama Chökyi Sengé) in French — their brilliance and mastery of their respective languages would magnify Rinpoché's words, giving them an exquisite quality that in no way distorted either what he had said or how he had said it. To hear those two translate for Rinpoché was to have heard his words expressed to perfection. However, even when they were not available for full-time translation and the job fell to me by default during the last years of Rinpoché's life, I was very often aware that Rinpoché's words alone, simply repeated in another language, were accurate darts that pierced the hearts of everyone present.

Kalu Rinpoché's teaching was exclusively Buddhist: he stressed the taking of refuge, the cultivation of the wish to attain enlightenment for the benefit of all beings, and meditation on the bodhisattva of compassion, All-Seeing One (known as *Avalokiteshvara* in Sanskrit, *Chenrézi* in Tibetan, or *Kuan Yin* in Chinese). He also repeated everywhere that he sincerely believed that all religions and spiritual paths lead to the same goal. He compared humanity's different faiths to the variety of restaurants one finds in a city: although hunger is the same worldwide, no one cuisine satisfies everyone. He was quite aware and accepting of the fact that all he had to offer — the rather exotic fare of Tibetan Buddhism — was not to everyone's taste.

Kalu Rinpoché was content to encourage faith in general and open-minded practice of Buddhism in particular, but when talking to Buddhists, he would invariably seem to say the opposite of what was expected of him. To dry and disciplined Zen Buddhists, he launched into rich descriptions of the pure lands and opulent visualized offerings. To straitlaced Chinese Buddhists, he described the glorious origins of the Buddha's teachings of the tantras — a king who had faith in the Buddha but would only practice his teachings if this didn't interfere with his daily routine of making love with five hundred queens during the day and another five hundred at night. To meditation-oriented and "liberated" Americans, he stressed karma, cause, and effect; and the many benefits of celibacy. To scholars, he would recount the life stories of yogis such as Milarepa or Naropa. To gung-ho practitioners, he advised putting meditation texts and prayer beads aside to look directly into the mind. And for just about everyone, everywhere, who heard Kalu Rinpoché speak a few times, he painted a detailed and gruesome picture of life in the hells, something no one wanted to hear. In short, he took it upon himself to remind everyone of the whole of the Buddha's teaching beyond each person's chosen and comfortable specialty. He had a knack for identifying a person's or a group's strengths and weaknesses. He would admiringly acknowledge the first and, on the subject of the second, he would leave an indelible memory of whatever a person or group habitually ignored or discounted in their approach to Buddhism or to life. Under those circumstances, it was surprising that anyone ever invited Rinpoché back for a second visit, but he was not only respected, he was deeply loved.

I always admired Kalu Rinpoché's access to himself, to all his states. He was comfortable being a child: he could be curious, naughty, playful, questioning, or struck with wonder. One of the first stories I heard before meeting him was of his having gotten lost in a huge department store in downtown Vancouver. Those who had accompanied him searched every floor and every department for the then-66-year-old unilingual Tibetan man in monk's robes. They eventually found him sitting on the floor at play with children in the toy department. During that first visit to the West (1971-72), he played on the stairs of his first meditation center with a "slinky" and in his room with a laugh box. He amused himself with toys all his life — hand puppets, wind-up dolls, masks. During his last few years, he added to the headaches of his personal secretary, Lama Gyaltsen, by insisting that the toys he collected in foreign countries be added to their already mountainous baggage, to be stored back home at the monastery, where they remained until his reincarnation was recognized.

Rinpoché was also comfortable being an adolescent: he could be adventuresome, willing to learn or to try new things, anarchic, vigorous, and joyful. He was comfortable being a young adult: he could be confident, energetic, dedicated, imaginative, bold, thoughtful, and charismatic. He was comfortable being a middle-aged man: he could be steady, careful, precise, conscientious, unhurried, and proud and attentive to his projects. Also like a middle-aged man, he could come home at the end of a long day's work, kick off his shoes, take his shirt off, and sit around in his monk underwear, relax, tell jokes and stories, eat foods he knew weren't good for him, and watch shows on television or video that he would gladly admit were awful.

Kalu Rinpoché was also comfortable with himself as an old man, and this is how most people first experienced him. He had reached the end of a life fully lived, and had nothing else to do but to give as much of himself as he could to anyone who needed his help. He lived without personal ambition, accepted each day as a blessing, greeted each new encounter as a gift, and routinely forgot almost everyone's name, be it Tibetan or foreign, be it of a close disciple or that of a stranger. But he never forgot a face or the conversations he had with any of the thousands of individuals he met, regardless of distances of time or space. He could recall each and every person, Tibetan or foreigner; those he had met yesterday at the monastery or those he had met ten years ago at the other end of the world. Before meeting him, I had assumed that the mind aged with the body: his never did, not even in the slightest. He exuded an old man's appreciation, affection, and best wishes for all his treasured acquaintances: they, his students and friends from around the globe, were the heart and the jewels of his life, and I am sure he died as he had lived, feeling great love and hope for the happiness and well-being of each and every one.

The Last Days of Kalu Rinpoché's Life

Two days after Kalu Rinpoché's death, I wrote the following account of his last days for the community of his students and friends worldwide. At that time, Rinpoché was still sitting in his final meditation — his breathing and heart had stopped, but his skin had not stiffened; he looked as if he was asleep. The next morning, after three days of *tukdam* (the Tibetan word for this state, although it literally is the honorific word for *meditation*), he finally passed away.

Lama Kalu Rinpoché passed away May 10 at 3:00 in the afternoon, at his monastery in Sonada, India. The fact that this news was received with disbelief by all of us is testimony to how present Rinpoché was among us until the final moments of his life.

Here is an account of the events of the last month, as I have seen them:

Rinpoché had been planning to visit Southeast Asia, Australia, and New Zealand during this spring. As his interpreter and sometime travel coordinator, I had become used to an element of unpredictability in Rinpoché's plans, but this spring's program was going relatively smoothly. The rule was that those of us working directly for him, his "mandala" of attendants, had to do our very best without any expectation that what seemed so sure today would be the case tomorrow. Rinpoché was first and foremost a yogi without personal ambition. His attention was on the needs of those who needed his help; he had no master plan, or any hidden agenda. We had to learn to serve someone who was responding to others' needs that were far more important than our small-minded satisfaction with a firm schedule for tomorrow's or next month's events. Still, all was going well, and Rinpoché was looking forward to his travels.

Two to three weeks before our intended day of departure from India to Malaysia, it became obvious to me that Rinpoché's health had deteriorated beyond what was normal for him in India. One evening, after talking with him as he was lying in bed, I spoke with Lama Gyaltsen, his "secretary" for want of a better word in any language to say "right-hand man," "confidant," "beloved shadow," "indispensable friend," and "devoted disciple" all at the same time. Gyaltsen said that he had the same thought that I had: we should go to Singapore before traveling to Malaysia, in order to give Rinpoché some time to rest and to see doctors if necessary. It was a very feasible plan. We had the time, Rinpoché was relatively fit, and our flight was already routed through Singapore. In spite of our requests to Rinpoché, he was firm in his wish to stay in Sonada until the last moment. We gave up asking after a couple of days, not knowing that this was the last real opportunity Rinpoché had to leave without it being a life-threatening gamble.

Ten days later, during the morning of April 4, Rinpoché found that his body was shaking uncontrollably. A doctor was summoned from Darjeeling: he advised Rinpoché be taken to a hospital on the plains, some seventy kilometers away and 2000 meters lower in elevation. This was done right away. The next morning I visited Rinpoché at a tiny clinic where a small room had been found for him; the main hospital had been full. He was sitting up, cross-legged, but had a tube in one nostril feeding him oxygen. He smiled as we talked, his eyes sparkling with his characteristic sense of humor. He may have been feeling weak or in pain but I didn't then, or ever, sense that he

suffered. He was too gentle, his sense of humor too enlightened, or all-encompassing, for him to take his own situation
personally.

I was there talking to him because I was to leave to Calcutta
at noon, a trip originally planned to renew my Indian visa. Now,
however, I was to communicate messages from Rinpoché to
his disciples in Southeast Asia. His expressed plan at that point
was to go to Singapore to consult the doctors there, to rest, and
then to continue his scheduled trip.

What concerned me at the time was not so much Rinpoché's
health crisis, which seemed minor compared to previous ones
over the last years, but his emaciation. Rinpoché has always
been thin, in spite of eating large amounts of food at banquets
in his honor: "We're not eating to make ourselves happy; we're
eating to make them happy!" was his admonishment to me as
I would pick apathetically at the umpteenth course. We became
used to the fact that his thinness and lack of appetite didn't
prevent him from doing the work of a man half his age. Looking through a *Time* magazine in Los Angeles this last winter,
he pointed to a picture of a man starving in a famine-stricken
region of Africa. "He looks like me!" he laughed. While that
was true — he would relax without wearing a shirt, a study in
skin and bones — wasn't he exhausting us as we tried to keep
up with him while he remained composed and with energy
to spare? This day at the clinic, however, he lifted his under-
skirt to thigh level for the doctor's examination. He had, in a
short time, crossed over the line from bare-wire spareness to
emaciation.

I left soon after and from Calcutta made one call which
Rinpoché hadn't requested but which seemed essential: to Situ
Rinpoché. Kalu Rinpoché's unquestioning respect for Situ
Rinpoché's advice had been proven to me time and again over
the years, and I felt it was appropriate to inform him of
Rinpoché's condition. I returned to Rinpoché's bedside a couple
of days later with a three-page letter that had been faxed that

morning from Situ Rinpoché. Rinpoché read it quickly, touched it to his forehead in respect, then reread it. I returned to Calcutta the next morning to relay the message to Rinpoché's centers worldwide that Situ Rinpoché advised Rinpoché's students to recite collectively one hundred million long Vajrasattva mantras, and as many long Amitayus mantras as possible.

By this time, Rinpoché was resting in a different clinic, in a large air-conditioned room. He had needed oxygen on the first day only and remained without it until the last. He seemed slightly weak but not enough to cause any immediate concern. The doctors had advised Rinpoché against traveling: his lungs' weakness was affecting his heart. His old foe, tuberculosis, had returned. There was too much risk in air travel, they said. Their prescription included rest, and more food, if possible. Rinpoché was still planning to travel and wanted to simply postpone his departure for a week. This seemed impossible to us, but he didn't want to disappoint those whom he had promised to visit. Finally, in spite of our insistence that he consider his health foremost, he decided that he would travel to Taiwan and Malaysia after having rested for one month, divided between India and Singapore. As always, his wishes prevailed.

Rinpoché returned to Sonada May 5, ostensibly because of the increasing heat on the plains. By this time the doctors had advised Rinpoché to rest completely for a number of months, not to teach or give empowerments, and to keep visits at an absolute minimum. All plans for travel were off until Rinpoché went to Singapore and was given a go-ahead from doctors there.

Rinpoché returned to the monastery late in the afternoon. The fog limited visibility to about twenty feet at most. We knew Rinpoché had arrived by the sound of Tibetan horns piercing the mist. The two horns preceded Rinpoché, who was carried up the steep path to his house, seated upright on a sedan chair made to be carried by six monks. Home again, Rinpoché scheduled a time the next day for all the monks of the monastery and Western visitors to see him, although it was made clear beforehand that questions were not permitted. I have been told that he sat upright and was fully engaged from start to finish, even asking after the health of others, on occasion. After that, Rinpoché followed the doctors' advice and refused all interviews. Doctors came to examine Rinpoché; however, no unusual concern showed in anyone's demeanor. Lama Gyaltsen was relaxed and smiling; everything was going as well as could be expected. No one seemed to doubt that, as had happened before, a little rest was all that was necessary before Rinpoché would resume his activity.

On May 10, very early in the morning, Rinpoché's physical situation became seriously worse. A car was sent at two in the morning to make the two-and-a-half-hour descent to the plains to bring a specialist. Another was sent later to bring a doctor from Darjeeling, an hour away.

I was called in to Rinpoché's bedside at eight-thirty that morning. As I did prostrations, Rinpoché looked over and said my name, but then his eyes rolled back and he closed them. I was told that since the early morning his eyes had been like that — even that amount of attention was too much. It was Lama Gyaltsen and Bokar Rinpoché who had called for me. Bokar Rinpoché, the retreat master of Rumtek Monastery, Kalu Rinpoché's monastery, and the Kalachakra retreat at his own monastery called Shambhala, may be unknown to many of you. It speaks volumes about his qualities to say that he is Kalu Rinpoché's main disciple, his Dharma heir. He asked me to call Jamgon Rinpoché,[4] then at Rumtek, to ask him to come to Sonada that day, as soon as possible, to do prayers and meditations to prolong Rinpoché's life. I went right away to Darjeeling to do so.

It may seem strange that I have mentioned, as here, going elsewhere to make a phone call. Kalu Rinpoché steadfastly refused to have a phone installed at the monastery or in the homes of disciples nearby. Even if there had been a phone, it would have been of little use. At the main phone office in Darjeeling the phone call to Jamgon Rinpoché took an hour to complete, even with the best cooperation of the employees of the phone company. Even then, the connection was bad. I shouted the message to the lama on the other end, hoping that he could hear me better than I could him. I sent a telegram to Situ Rinpoché as an international call must be booked seven or eight hours in advance, with no promise that the connection would be audible. (Hence the trips to Calcutta previously, where half-hour or hour waits and better connections seem luxurious.)

I then tried to call Rumtek again to confirm that the message had been received. A couple of hours later I was able to get through and was told that, yes, Jamgon Rinpoché was on his way.

It was approximately 2:30 PM when I returned to Rinpoché's house. The doctor from the plains had long since arrived, bringing with him an electrocardiogram machine. He had determined that Rinpoché had suffered a serious heart attack. He advised that Rinpoché be moved back to the plains to be put in intensive care. Baggage had been packed and put in the cars. When it came time for Rinpoché to leave it was impossible for him to leave his room, so I was told. I do not know what happened at that time, but the doctor told me that he had concluded that it was too risky for Rinpoché to leave. We should wait forty-eight hours, a critical period, so he said.

Rinpoché had been moved from his large receiving room to a small antechamber which he had used as a bedroom in other years. By this time he was receiving oxygen through one nostril and glucose intravenously. He was quite conscious, but breathing took much of his energy; his lungs, according to the doctor, were forty percent functional. We moved suitcases and boxes out of the room to make more space and moved the bed from the wall to make a little space on all four sides. As we were moving back and forth between rooms I noticed on a shelf the long-life vase that Rinpoché told me had belonged to Jamgon Kongtrul the Great, his previous incarnation. He too had lived into his eighties, and I hoped that the connection of having the vase, and the three large statues that are in Rinpoché's main room, the three gods of long life, would prolong Rinpoché's life even further.

I talked to the doctor and then communicated his feelings to Bokar Rinpoché and to Khenpo Lodru Donyu, the abbot of the monastery. At that time, besides the four of us, Lama Gyaltsen, Drolkar (Gyaltsen's wife), Lama Sonam Tsering (a young lama who had been attending Rinpoché during his hospitalization), Ani Choga (Kalu Rinpoché's sister), and a Nepalese nurse were present in the two rooms with Rinpoché.

For the last few days, Rinpoché had been lying lifted at an angle, as a measure to prevent congestion. He now wanted to sit up, but this proved too uncomfortable. He then lay back in a half-upright position, breathing quickly from the effort of trying to sit up. Either in the movement of the bed or in Rinpoché's movement, the intravenous tube had slipped out of his arm. It was not replaced.

At that moment Chadral Rinpoché came into the outer room. He is one of the greatest lamas of the Nyingma tradition, and one of Kalu Rinpoché's close friends and disciples. He is in his seventies, but despite a lifetime of meditation practice to the disregard of his own well-being, his health seems excellent. One of his main monasteries is in Ghoom, a few miles away from Sonada. He had been summoned early that morning, had come, and had left at the same time I went to Darjeeling. Upon his return he went straight into Rinpoché's little room, where he was joined by Bokar Rinpoché, Lama Gyaltsen, Khenpo Lodru Donyu, Lama Sonam Tsering, the nurse, and Drolkar. After a very few minutes, Drolkar came out, moved to tears. She joined Ani Choga, the doctor, and me in the outer room.

I do not know how long the next sequence of events took. Perhaps five minutes, perhaps ten. The doctor and I were in the middle of a conversation about what possibilities there were for Rinpoché's care when the nurse summoned him into the room. Perhaps two or three minutes later, the nurse left Rinpoché's room and whispered, "His respiration has stopped." Drolkar asked what she had said; I wouldn't answer. I couldn't believe that he wouldn't start breathing again. A few minutes later, Lama Sonam Tsering and the doctor came out: the doctor said, "He has expired." Drolkar heard this, then left the room. I repeated in Tibetan what he had said to Rinpoché's sister. In Tibetan one says, "He has gone to the pure lands."[5]

I could hear Chadral Rinpoché's deep voice intone some verses addressed to Rinpoché. We sat in silence until Bokar Rinpoché, Khenpo Lodru Donyu, and Lama Gyaltsen came back into the room.

Rinpoché's passing happened very peacefully, in an atmosphere of calm and gentleness. He was at home, in the center of his own world. We had wished Rinpoché to go to the West or to Singapore to recover. But it became impossible, even, I think, if there had been a group of doctors aiding and accompanying him. Everything physically possible was done for Rinpoché. The lamas, monks, and nuns of his monastery would have gladly given their own breath to prolong his life. Yet no one really expected him to pass away. He was so vital, so present, in all of our lives up to the last day. In fact, he still is.

He sits now in meditation posture in his little room. Jamgon Rinpoché, Chadral Rinpoché, and Bokar Rinpoché are doing prayers in the outer room all day. The lamas, monks, nuns, and friends, both Western and Tibetan, are doing prayers in the temple. We are waiting for Rinpoché to leave: his breathing and heart have stopped, but, as is said in Tibetan, his meditation is not finished. When the signs of his inner passing appear, a different set of prayers will be done until the end of a forty-nine-day period.

I hope that this account brings you all closer to Rinpoché at this time. May we all realize a prayer that Rinpoché was fond of repeating at the end of public events:

During all my lifetimes may I never be separated from
   the authentic lama.
May I thereby enjoy the splendor of the Dharma,
Come to perfectly embody the qualities of the paths and
   stages of awakening,
And quickly attain the state of enlightenment of the
   Buddha Vajradhara.

Kalu Rinpoché's Return

A year and a half later, on September 17, 1990, Drolkar gave
birth to a child. He was a remarkably happy baby; he virtually
never cried. Instead, he smiled and laughed all day long. I remarked to Drolkar that everyone would want to have a baby
like hers, his disposition was so strikingly sunny. Everyone
called him Bu-trook ("little child"). Tibetan parents do not usually name their own children, and this was no exception. Lama
Gyaltsen and Drolkar decided to use the name given by the
first high lama who met their son. Appropriately, it was Bokar
Rinpoché, Kalu Rinpoché's spiritual heir, who gave him his first
name: Poon-tsok Chö-pel, meaning "magnificent one who
spreads the Buddha's teaching."

It was not long before some people decided on their own
that this boy was the reincarnation of Kalu Rinpoché. A short
time after the birth, one of Rinpoché's well-loved and most
trusted Western disciples, Joseph Duane, visited to greet the
new arrival. I recall being shocked that he, an international cor-
porate lawyer with three children of his own, treated the tiny
infant in a crib with total conviction that this was Kalu Rinpoché
returned to life. He was bolder than most of us (most of us
confined our thoughts on the subject to "Wouldn't it be wonderful if it were Rinpoché's reincarnation"), but he was quite
right, of course.

Word from high lamas was not long in coming. Chadral
Rinpoché, Kalu Rinpoché's friend, was the first reliable and
respected meditation master to express the opinion publicly
that little "Bu-trook" was more than just a delightful addition to
our lives at Kalu Rinpoché's monastery. Later, Tai Situpa visited

the monastery and told Lama Gyaltsen privately that he wished to ask the Dalai Lama to confirm his impression that the child was Kalu Rinpoché's reincarnation. Lama Gyaltsen carried a letter from Tai Situpa to Dharamsala and very quickly received His Holiness' firm confirmation. Moreover, the Dalai Lama promised to visit the young reincarnation at his monastery.

This was great and welcome news: Lama Gyaltsen, who had devotedly served Kalu Rinpoché almost every day for forty years, and Drolkar, who had accompanied, served, and fed him for the last twelve years of his life, seemed the ideal parents for the new reincarnation. We could all attest that even though they had indications that their son was a tulku, they hadn't made a big deal of it. They gave him the care and attention that any loving parents would.

Drolkar, Rinpoché's mother, is a hard-working and humble woman. After an early marriage and divorce, she single-handedly raised three daughters, ran a business, and built a fine home for her family before marrying Lama Gyaltsen. At forty, she is a grandmother who wants her two daughters still in school to continue their education as long as they possibly can, to enjoy the opportunity for an education she feels she lacked. "Don't end up stupid like your mother!" she advises them in sincere humility. This from a woman who has traveled many times around the world feeding and caring for Kalu Rinpoché, possesses a lively mind always interested in learning and understanding the world, and speaks five languages fluently — her native Bhutanese, Tibetan, Nepalese, English, and French — without a day of formal study in any: she was too busy working and providing for her family.

The child's father, Lama Gyaltsen, needs no introduction for anyone who met Kalu Rinpoché during the last forty years of his life: Lama Gyaltsen was always there, Rinpoché's most devoted and dedicated disciple after Bokar Rinpoché, and the one person to whom Rinpoché would consistently confide his innermost feelings. A slow, careful, methodical man by nature, Lama Gyaltsen has become cosmopolitan from years of accompanying Kalu Rinpoché many times around the world. He is always patient, gentle, diplomatic, and sensitive to others' feelings. Most relevant to his role as the father of a reincarnate master, he is discreet and harbors no personal ambitions. For those who know him well, Lama Gyaltsen commands deep respect as a person who genuinely practices his spiritual path, as a warm and openhearted human being, and, like his wife, as an exemplary parent.

Three leaders of the Kagyu lineage officiated at Kalu Rinpoché's enthronement: Tai Situpa, Gyaltsab Rinpoché, and Bokar Rinpoché. Hundreds attended, including two television crews from France and a wall of photographers. As we waited outside the temple to be allowed to enter, a circular rainbow around the sun appeared on the eastern horizon. I had not seen or heard of one at the monastery since Rinpoché's death (one appeared at the end of the forty-nine-day period after his death), nor have I seen or heard of one appearing since the enthronement: it seemed a small special sign marking and linking the two events. When little Rinpoché, then two and a half, entered and was placed on the throne, he was faced with the press and their intense lights: he lay down on his throne beside Tai Situpa and appeared to sleep until the camera lights were dimmed, after the main part of the ceremony. He then sat up and participated in the blessing of each person present as they filed past him, and later performed his own version of "lama dances" before hundreds of people in the courtyard of the monastery, as an impromptu part of the celebration after the enthronement.

One month after this event, His Holiness the Dalai Lama visited Kalu Rinpoché's monastery and performed a hair-cutting ceremony, after which he gave a short talk. Nothing in the Tibetan world is more important than a visit by the Dalai Lama; nothing is even remotely comparable. We say casually in the West that he is "the spiritual and political leader of the Tibetan people," but to share the event of his visit with Tibetans is to appreciate that he is far closer to and more intimately loved by his people than our leaders are by us. Yet he embodies every bit of the power and prestige that a culture can invest in its president, prime minister, king or queen, and spiritual chief. To the Tibetans, he is the lama of lamas, and the king of kings. I mention this so you can better understand the general horror which greeted the sight of the infant Kalu Rinpoché, seated on a tiny seat below and in front of His Holiness, refusing to sit still. Rinpoché's parents usually let him come and go as he pleases, but the Dalai Lama's visit was a serious exception. Despite desperate, pleading, insistent whispers on the part of those seated close to Rinpoché, he stood up, by this time having distracted the attention of most of the audience and finally that of the Dalai Lama himself. Rinpoché stepped down from his seat, turned his back on Tibet's highest authority, fumbled with his little monk-cape, and then turned around and did full-length prostrations to the Dalai Lama. His Holiness roared with laughter, said it was a very good sign, and had Rinpoché carried before him. Then, in the most respectful and intimate gesture that lamas use, he touched foreheads with the child he had confirmed as Kalu Rinpoché the year before.

The Young Reincarnate Master Meets the World

Both the Dalai Lama and Tai Situpa have advised that Rinpoché's education begin around the age of six, as both have expressed their feeling that both Tibetan and Western parents push their children too soon out of childhood. All the same, Rinpoché is enjoying a childhood quite unlike that of others his age: Tai Situpa has asked that he use these years to travel around the world to visit the students and meditation centers of his last life. His journey began last year, 1994, with a trip to Hong Kong, Taiwan, China, and Tibet. According to Rinpoché's father, the visit to Tibet was Rinpoché's own idea: he learned a popular Tibetan song which includes the line, "How happy I would be if I went to Tibet!" and would sing it often with strong feeling. He also repeatedly asked his parents to take him to meet Karmapa, the young reincarnate leader of the Kagyu tradition. They gave him his wish. The meeting, in Tsurpu Monastery close to Lhasa, was a great success: the nine-year-old Karmapa and the three-year-old Kalu Rinpoché found they shared more than a common calling as reincarnate lamas — they played together for hours with model cars on the flat roof of the main temple. A week later, in Chengdu, China, Kalu Rinpoché met Dudjom Rinpoché, the reincarnation of the leader of the Nyingma tradition. This turned out to be a very moving encounter — after playing wildly for a few minutes, Kalu Rinpoché asked for some money from his father, then did three full-length prostrations and gave the money as an offering to Dudjom Rinpoché, a little boy his own age, then three years old. For better or for worse, little Kalu Rinpoché acts independently and has a mind of his own which no one pretends to fathom.

After we left Tibet and China, Rinpoché, his parents, and a group of lamas from his monastery visited thirty of Rinpoché's meditation centers in Europe. We spent most of five months in France, and made short visits to Spain, Belgium, Denmark, and Italy. This turned out to be a very enjoyable, touching, and inspiring family reunion for the thousands who knew Kalu Rinpoché in the past. Many came to see Rinpoché out of curiosity, simply to see the young child who bears the name of someone they had known, loved, and respected. In spite of minimal expectations, they found that meeting the child reawakened or touched something deep within them that Kalu Rinpoché had many years before. That was a very typical reaction. Those who had never met the elder Kalu Rinpoché were most often charmed by the child and impressed by his ease, calm, and attentiveness before any number of people, for up to five hundred people attended some events.

At three years old, Rinpoché did no teaching, but he loved to communicate through dance. As soon as he began to watch videos as an infant, he would ask endlessly for one and one only — that of lama dances. Since that time he has copied what he has seen as best he can, for none of his lama babysitters, most of whom are proficient dancers, want to begin teaching

The new incarnation of Kalu Rinpoché, born September 17, 1990.
(Photo: Alison Wright)

him. Left to himself, he watches his video and the monks' per-
formances and has developed his own style. His parents are
not eager to have him begin any formal training, dance included: they prefer him to explore things on his own, but at
least they have had a traditional lama-dance costume sewn to
fit his diminutive size. Rinpoché would ask to perform for the
public in different meditation centers in Europe, always
spontaneously.

He usually attacks his numbers seriously and with verve,
sometimes performing just one "lama dance," sometimes more.
Stage fright seems not to be an emotion he is acquainted with,
but neither does he abuse the attention he commands: sometimes his dances are very brief, as if that was all he had on his
mind to express on that occasion. On one very memorable occasion, he danced three times (he exits between dances), for
the residents of his largest European center, Kagyu Ling in central France. Ordinarily he dances quickly and expressively, and
his second dance of this performance was particularly lively.
On his third entrance, he seemed to be moving in slow motion;
he did a long, fluid, sensitive dance, holding a vajra (Tibetan
ritual scepter) in his right hand, sometimes wielding it, sometimes presenting it to his small audience. His other dances had
been greeted with laughing and clapping: this time, the room
was still. We were rapt. He exited stepping backward, bowing,
holding the vajra at its center, arm extended. The vajra is a symbol of perfect skill, clarity, and precision. I prefer to not read
things into Rinpoché's gestures, but on that occasion I had the
unavoidable sensation of having witnessed a masterful performance, of having been shown part of the depth, stillness, and
clarity of mind through his dance. Perhaps it was an accident,
but the very least one can say without contradiction is that on
that day he showed a sense of timing and stage presence that
are unusual in completely self-trained three-year-olds.

It is easy to misinterpret the foreignness of lama dances,
but little Rinpoché also enjoyed dancing to Western music in

Western styles. During our travels, if the schedule permitted and the mood was right, a celebration would erupt. (It is remarkable how much good rock-and-roll and rhythm and blues can be found at a moment's notice in Kalu Rinpoché's meditation retreat centers deep in the French or Spanish countryside.) It took no time at all for Rinpoché to get the beat and to dance the night away with an unlikely crew of Tibetan lamas and European men and women. One moment for me was particularly memorable: the last night of our visit to a retreat center near Montpellier, in southern France. Rinpoché was in high spirits and was bursting with joy while dancing. One of the many who danced with him that night was the young lama who leads the retreat center, Lama Sonam Tsering, Kalu Rinpoché's attendant at his bedside at his death. For him, as for so many of us, whatever sorrow from Rinpoché's death still lingered was greatly eased by that beaming, rambunctious small boy.

I have heard that some people, amazed at this young boy's charm and ease, are convinced that he cannot even be a child born in 1990, that he must have been born before Kalu Rinpoché's death and brought forward to take his place. I sympathize with that view, for although I've known him since soon after his birth (definitely September 17, 1990) and know that he's a child, in my mind I can't help but think of him as a young man.

He was of course showered with toys, and he littered the interiors of meditation centers from Brussels to Barcelona with his playing. Yet minutes after being accosted by a small masked crusader-terrorist answering only to the name of Batman, one could find the same three-year-old on a throne whose stillness, patience, and presence were breathtaking. Everyone who visits Rinpoché sees these two aspects, the child and the master. I do not see these as contradictory: yes, the Dalai Lama and others who are responsible for his education expect him to follow their example and become a Buddhist master and teacher. But I feel they want his education to bring awareness and precision to what is already fully present in the child. His state as a child is not seen by those around him as something to be overcome, discarded, disowned, or discredited.

The child in the late Kalu Rinpoché never died, nor was it ever repressed. The new child Kalu Rinpoché is both a child and a reincarnate master. He sits on thrones before large crowds and displays alert, still, and contained attention. He participates in rituals, playing proficiently at age three the same hand-drum and bell that his predecessor did, and he gives his blessing to lines of hundreds of persons at a time. These things can be learned, although I have never seen him taught them. I have seen him act this way since he was recognized at one and a half years of age.

The Tulku's Father Meets the Media

The one negative side to our European visit was that played by the media. Rinpoché's visit was made in response to invitations from his meditation centers — his former students wanted to meet the child before he begins his education, after which time, like any child in the world, he will have only a short vacation each year for rest or travel. The media had not figured in our plans, but they were welcomed at all public events. Kalu Rinpoché and his centers had always been treated very respectfully by the press and television in Europe, yet our relationship with the press turned out to be one of the more troubling aspects of Kalu Rinpoché's visit to the West.

A couple of weeks after we arrived in France, a local television station's report on Rinpoché was picked up and included in the evening news by two of the three national networks. I had often heard, and now believe, that nothing in this world truly exists unless it has been on television. What had begun as a family affair, a happy meeting shared by the members of the Buddhist community, turned into an Event and Rinpoché into a darling of the media who seemed determined to turn him into a Star.

Little Kalu Rinpoché never got "bad press." Quite the contrary — he was adored and celebrated in every printed article and televised report that appeared. If we had been looking for publicity, it would have been a dream come true, but that was far from the case. Lama Gyaltsen would have me translate for the interviews he reluctantly gave. Each time, he began by saying that he felt the media's attention to his son was misplaced, that he would be happy for his son to become famous later in his life, if that renown was due to recognition of his qualities or talents he had independently put to use for the service of mankind. In the meantime, Lama Gyaltsen said he felt uncomfortable both as a parent and as a Buddhist at the attention his son was receiving from outside the Buddhist community. To the inevitable question "Did you know your son was a reincarnate lama before he was recognized?" Lama Gyaltsen would answer, "As Buddhists, we don't talk about our experiences, and besides, whatever my own impressions might have been, they mean nothing compared to the word of such masters as His Holiness the Dalai Lama and Tai Situpa. I trust them much more than my own thoughts." And to "How has your life changed?" he would say, and I think this is the key to understanding the atmosphere in which, ideally, every reincarnate lama is placed after his or her recognition, "I don't have the feeling that my life has changed at all. I am sixty years old now; I have spent the last fifty years of my life serving Kalu Rinpoché. I don't know whether that is due to karma, to personal connections, or to positive aspirations I made in other lifetimes, but I expect that I will spend the rest of my life serving him as best I can."

I do not mean to detract from Lama Gyaltsen if I point out that in articulating these feelings he was giving voice to his culture's attitudes. The peoples of the Himalayas love their spiritual leaders, but they do not want or expect them to become stars in India, Asia, or the West. The hundreds of reincarnate masters alive today show tremendous discipline in following their culture's precepts. They do not make a big deal of themselves; they do not place themselves above their teachers or their people. Tibetan tulkus are encouraged at every stage of their education and training to respect and preserve the Buddha's teaching and to use their capabilities to serve their community and the world. They are discouraged from seeking unearned recognition in the outside world; instead, they are raised to feel concern for and to serve each and every being — human, animal, god, ghost, or demon — who crosses their path. The accumulation of fame and fortune is not on their agenda.

Imagine, if you can, such persons as the Dalai Lama, Dudjom Rinpoché, Dilgo Kyentsé Rinpoché, Sakya Trizin, Karmapa, and so many others among the great reincarnate masters our generation has been honored to know. In classical literary Tibetan, their names are sometimes prefaced by an expression which means "the name which is difficult to say aloud." This refers to the overwhelming emotion an ordinary person feels when he or she recalls these masters and fully remembers their qualities before speaking their names. Yet however extraordinary they are, these masters never stand apart from their roots in Buddhism and their communities. They never "cash in" on their greatness, even to simply retire to a comfortable private life in their old age, without the irritations of students and responsibilities. This is a thousand-year-old tradition of dignity and humility, which Lama Gyaltsen belongs to and which Kalu Rinpoché will be raised in. In the end I don't think Kalu Rinpoché will be harmed by the media attention. The media has a notoriously tiny span of attention, but even at its most persistent, it cannot undo the influence of Rinpoché's cultural and spiritual background. And most particularly, at this stage in his life, Rinpoché's parents are the surest guarantors of a sane environment for him.

At the same time, the love and attention that are now showered on the little Rinpoché (and other infant reincarnate masters) by Buddhists throughout the world is, to me, natural and unthreatening. There is such a wealth of love, wisdom, gentleness, and purity of purpose in every corner of the Buddhist world that I do not fear Kalu Rinpoché's exposure to the world. He has proved himself able to meet the world as a young tulku, while remaining intent on enjoying the experience of childhood.

PART ONE

The Recognition of
Reincarnate Masters —
An Interview with Tai Situpa

The Recognition of Reincarnate Masters

Shortly after my teacher, Kalu Rinpoché, died in 1989, I visited Tai Situ Rinpoché at his monastery in northwest India. Although that was the first time I asked Tai Situ Rinpoché for permission to translate this text, it was not until 1992, when our monastery was preparing for the enthronement ceremony of the child Tai Situpa had recognized (and the Dalai Lama had confirmed) as the reincarnation of Kalu Rinpoché, that I began work on this translation. I was interested in this text because it described enthronement, the first major public event in the life of a reincarnate lama. Many of the great teachers who guided my generation of Buddhists during the late sixties and seventies and passed away in the eighties have been reborn in the late eighties and early nineties and are now being enthroned, reinstalled in their former institutions. To answer my own and others' questions concerning this new phase of our lives with Tibet's tulkus, I undertook this translation with Tai Situ Rinpoché's blessing.

Tai Situpa travels throughout the world to foster spiritual awakening through a wide range of activities which reflect his enormous talent that flows far beyond what we might associate with a Buddhist monk and teacher. He is an artist, a writer, an administrator, a spiritual guide, and, above all, a citizen of the world. But he is also a deeply traditional keeper of the flame of centuries of spiritual awakening in the Himalayas: he has recognized over a hundred infants as reincarnate masters. These have been found according to his directions, have been enthroned, and are being educated. They will ensure the continuity of Buddhism for the next generation of Buddhists in the Himalayan region and for many around the world. It was principally for this reason that I wished to interview him for this book.

This interview took place on August 20, 1993, at Rumtek Monastery, near Gangtok, Sikkim, northeast India. We sat in a large room on the second floor of the monastery: Tai Situpa's reception room and office during the day, his bedroom at night. It was a simple but exquisite setting: the floors of the room were of a dark-colored polished wood, his and other monks' robes a deep wine, and lively, multicolored religious paintings framed in ornate brocade decorated the walls. But it was the golden yellow of his shirt and the sunlight filtered through curtains of the same color which suffused the room. His attendants' and messengers' constant coming and going reminded me that he was a very busy man, but he was relaxed: he made me feel as if we had all the time in the world. We spoke in English. Tai Situpa's command of English is impressive; his usage echoes the richly flavored blend of British, American, and Indian English one hears among Tibetans educated in India. He is sharp and quick-witted: he often answered questions before I had finished my sentence. He was thoughtful, serious, and forthcoming but laughed easily and often, often self-deprecatingly.

We began by speaking of the state some meditation masters (as well as some "ordinary persons") enter at death, a sort of suspended animation in which the person may rest for many days after the doctor proclaims the individual dead. He or she no longer breathes and has no heartbeat, but the skin remains supple and lifelike, the heart area warm, and the head upright. The Tibetans call this *tukdam* (*thugs dam*), an honorific word meaning "meditation." This state might be considered the first step in the process of death and rebirth of many reincarnate masters.

To better comprehend the process of death and rebirth of a reincarnate master, I asked many questions concerning the degree of choice exercised by the reincarnate master compared to the degree of choice we ordinary persons have over the circumstances of our rebirth. Tai Situpa then discussed the process of recognition and confirmation of the reborn masters.

Two comments from this interview seem to me to be particularly revealing of the Tibetan relationship to this system. First, the child is not expected to conform to the demands of a system; the onus is on the system to nourish the child and to respond to his or her needs.

> *Tai Situpa*: We cannot lock them [reincarnate masters] into this one, fixed situation, because everything might be perfect, but they intentionally try to manifest something not so perfect in order to make some benefit out of it. That could be. [page 75]

In other words, the Tibetans do not expect their system to remain static, no matter how ideal it might seem. Although the child might sometimes seem (and feel?) like a prisoner of the monastery, it is recognized that spiritual awakening is the innate potential of a human being, never that of any human invention, institutions included.

Second, there is no accepted central authority for recognizing reincarnate masters. Even the Dalai Lama's "spiritual authority" exists only inasmuch as Tibetans have faith in him. Tai Situpa refers here to the recognition of the latest reincarnation (the seventeenth) of the first reincarnate master of Tibet, the Karmapa:

> If they don't have faith and trust — you can see what's happened in the case of His Holiness Karmapa. You can see. Karmapa was born there [in eastern Tibet]; he was recognized through his own writing in the most historical, most traditional way, His Holiness the Dalai Lama was the supreme

authority [who gave confirmation to the recognition], and
he's already been enthroned in Tsurpu [Karmapa's main
monastery in central Tibet] for more than one year. Still,
some people don't want to believe. So if there's no faith, no
trust, no devotion, it doesn't work for them. [page 77]

The choice of candidate for Karmapa's title and throne remains an insoluble controversy, with two candidates proposed:
one supported by His Holiness the Dalai Lama, Tai Situpa, and
others; another, by Shamarpa and his circle of followers. Both
candidates have been enthroned: one in Tibet, the other in India. Both sides agree that there can be only one Karmapa (as is
the case with the Dalai Lama). Nevertheless, it is entirely possible that both sides would agree that both candidates are reincarnate masters, as few Tibetans imagine that great bodhisattvas
limit their activity in this world to just one manifestation. The
problem lies more in the realm of spiritual authority, a question that in the Tibetan world is multiple choice. There is one
simple answer—confidence in the Dalai Lama—and a multitude of less orthodox alternatives.

As unseemly as the present situation appears, it does not
seem to be unusual. Tibetan Buddhism is perhaps the most dis-
organized of organized religions. Its greatest wealth lies in the
quality of the traditions of philosophy and meditation that the
Tibetan masters have kept vibrantly alive. The masters' ranks
have been enriched continuously for centuries by the infant
reincarnate lamas recognized by such spiritual leaders as Tai
Situ Rinpoché. The name or title a tulku finally bears is a critical issue for those who live in the worldwide Tibetan neigh-
borhood, but the world at large only stands to gain from the
presence of bodhisattvas in the world, regardless of the names
they are given.

An Interview with Tai Situpa

Rumtek Monastery, Sikkim; August 20, 1993

THE PROCESS OF DEATH AND REBIRTH

Ngawang Zangpo: Let's start by talking about what happens to high lamas when they die. They go into a state the Tibetans call *tukdam* (literally, "meditation").

Tai Situpa: Tukdam doesn't have to be high lamas. *Tukdam* can also be done by low lamas [laughs] but, you know, good lamas. Good lamas who have done lots of meditation, and they recognize their minds; when they die, they go into a meditative state. It's a realization.

Q: Why do they stay in their bodies?

A: Because the body is very strongly connected with the mind. You cannot find anything that is closer to your mind than your own body. So when the mind is OK then the body for sure is OK... Temporarily [laughs].

Q: At this time, seen from the outside, they've died. On the inside, what are they doing?

The Twelfth Tai Situpa, Péma Donyö Nyinjé.
(Photo: Sherab Ling Buddhist Institute)

A: They're not doing anything. They've recognized the nature of mind. They have realization. Mind and body have separated: when that happens, they recognize it, and they realize.

Q: Some lamas who seem to us to be "high lamas" stay a very short time in this state.

A: That doesn't matter. "Long" or "short" has nothing to do with anything. It doesn't depend upon anything. It just means that the person's mind stays in that body for a long or short time after death.

Q: When Karmapa died did you expect him to enter *tukdam*?

A: No. We don't necessarily expect anyone to sit in that [state]. Karmapa did, but not necessarily. We don't necessarily *expect* it. Because this is a sign. But then he might not want [to give] a sign. In that way it doesn't really make much difference. If somebody doesn't have full control then if they are in a good meditative state [at death] and they realize [the nature of mind], then they will naturally enter *tukdam* without too much of their own choice. But if someone is highly enlightened and has more freedom then it doesn't have to be this way or that way, or any way, whichever way they choose. Like Karmapa: we will not expect, "Oh, he *must* sit in *tukdam*!" Not like that. But the sixteenth Karmapa did.

Q: Were you there at the time?

A: Yes.

Q: This was in the United States?

A: Yes. He died due to — I don't know the exact term — lots of fluid in the lungs or something. It's some kind of pneumonia. That's how he died.

Q: Because he died in a hospital, did you have to warn them beforehand that he would enter *tukdam*?

A: It was not like that. He was in the hospital, and the hospital doctors were trying their best to assist him. And then the doctors gave up, and we all had to accept that.

Q: But ordinarily in the West once a person dies the body must be taken by a service.

A: No, they left him. They left him in the same room because we showed them that he was in a meditative state and they were convinced.

Q: They were convinced?

A: Yes. Otherwise they would not have allowed [the body to remain there].

Q: They must have been surprised.

A: I think so. I think so.

Q: Apart from high ... good lamas, do some ordinary people — good practitioners — also enter *tukdam*?

A: Of course, of course, of course! If that person realizes the nature of mind during death.

Q: You say, "Of course!" but for us this is very unusual.

A: I don't know what is unusual [laughs].

Q: After this period of meditation is completed, what happens to this good lama or good practitioner?

A: Then that person has recognition of the nature of mind. That means the person is enlightened. At least recognizes the nature of mind. Close to the first level of bodhisattva. At least.

Q: Then after the period of time in the post-death meditative state — if it's a day, four days, three days, however many days — then what happens?

A: Usually not more than three days. Sometimes even [just] one day. Then the mind will go to wherever the person chooses: to be reborn again to help others, or to be reborn in a pure land, whatever.

Q: When ordinary persons die without recognition of the nature of mind, it is said that within forty-nine days they must take rebirth.

A: Forty-nine days is the maximum [period between lifetimes] for human beings on the planet Earth. Because of the body, because of the mind, because of many conditions. Maximum for a human being on this planet. When they die, forty-nine days from their death, they take entry into the next realm. Could be one second, three days, one day — anytime — but cannot be more than forty-nine days. But this does not cover others, including animals. This is the bardo according to humans.

Q: But for the person who has recognized the nature of mind, this does not apply?

A: Bardo [is something you undergo] by force. By the force of karma and everything. But the person who has stayed in *tukdam* has nothing to do with that. But we still do the rituals [for them after their death], all of that. There's nothing wrong with that. It's good. There can never be too much merit [laughs]!

Q: In the period between the time a lama has entered *tukdam* or has attained enlightenment and is reborn, can they be conscious of their students?

A: Definitely! Of course!

Q: Do they have a form at that point, or are they just mind, or does mind have a form?

A: Mind doesn't have a form as such, but if you wanted to use the concept "Are they somewhere?" of course they are there. At that point in time they are in their body. That's why their body is in *tukdam* [meditation] position.

Q: And after they have left their body, where do they go? Do they have a form?

A: Then wherever they go, that's where they are. They can go to heaven or to their next rebirth. Of course. They can move from one place to another. They are somewhere. But form is totally experiential. Form is according to our body, our eyes, our ears, our nose, our tongue. According to those [senses], we call [something] "form." But there is no such thing [in this case]. I don't think you can touch mind with your body. Somebody's mind. You cannot. But it is in a place. It moves from one place to another. It enters into the next realm, the next life. It will then have its own length of life.

Q: So if a lama, a tulku, doesn't take rebirth for a number of years, he or she is somewhere.

A: We don't know where he is: maybe in heaven, maybe doing something for someone in other places.

Q: Some students feel after their lama has died somehow closer to the lama, or they feel their lama's presence even stronger.

A: That sounds good!

Q: Is this just in their own minds or is this real?

A: I think that's impossible to differentiate [laughs]. Isn't it? [Points out the window.] Is the sky blue or blue the sky? [Laughs.] Yes. I think it's the same thing. The connection [between lama and student]. We can't differentiate these things.

CHOICE AND THE PROCESS OF REBIRTH

Q: How much choice do ordinary people have over where they're reborn, their circumstances?

A: They have all the choices. They have all the choices. Wherever they are born or whatever they will go through, good or bad or so-so. Everything is due to their own doing.

Q: Their own doing?

A: They have all the choice; we have all the choice. But once we have done something bad or something negative, then it's done. Of course one can confess, can purify it. And even once we have done something good we can also destroy it, contaminate it. But our own choice is there, of course.

Q: If I choose to be reborn in Hawaii, a very nice place, to very good parents.

A: Then you should do lots of good karma, you should accumulate lots of merit, you should purify lots of bad karma all your life. That's your choice [laughs]. But that is needed if you say, "I want to be reborn in Hawaii as a human being, in a very good family, in order to help lots of people and to develop myself." If you say that. Otherwise, in Hawaii there are lots of flies and worms and you know [laughs]. You can be reborn in Hawaii and not need so much merit [laughs]!

Q: Some people believe that whatever parents you have is because of your conscious choice. You've chosen somewhere — maybe in the bardo — you've chosen your parents.

A: No. You cannot. Conscious choice? Unconsciously, you can say you choose everything. You could go to a jail and find a real, convicted criminal and you can say [to him], "You choose to be here." I mean you can justify that by using all kinds of legal terms, but it doesn't mean he consciously wanted to be in that cell, he consciously wanted to be in trouble. I don't think so. He thought he would never be in trouble. He might have thought it possible, but he hoped he would get away with it. We cannot say "choice." If they are enlightened, yes, there is choice, but otherwise, no. That's, I think, a [mistaken] democratic concept of karma.

Q: If you have intense anger in one lifetime, are you reborn with that trait?

A: Definitely! Definitely! There was some red clay on top of the mountain during the monsoons, that red clay will be seen in the river below, so it is true. It continues. In one life we are one hundred percent compassionate, and in just the next life by some mistake we become very uncompassionate person? It's not like that. It continues.

Q: Is the cycle of life, death, and rebirth like a school? Do you learn through it? The next life doesn't help teach you not to be angry?

A: Um, well, that needs lots of merit. That's what it's all about. If you have merit: yes, of course.

Q: But otherwise it's not naturally that...

A: That because you're bad naturally that you become good? No. If there is merit, if there is cause and condition to be that way, it will work that way. If there's no cause and condition to be that way, it will not be that way. But ultimately, ultimately, we don't believe in karma. Because buddha-nature, the mind, has no limitation. Ultimately. But karma is the relative truth. So in order to overcome karma, your ultimate truth — realization — should be more powerful than your relative truth — karma. So if you become enlightened today it means you don't have to go through all that you have done for the past twenty-five billion lifetimes. It's all taken care of. Ten million centuries of darkness can be lighted [snaps fingers] by one candle in a second. Yeah?

Q: If a person has this enlightenment, they have complete choice over their life. There's no force of karma pushing them to be reborn? Just their own will?

A: Definitely, definitely! But you're not talking about Buddha's enlightenment. Buddha is beyond that.

Q: What level are we talking about?

A: We're talking about a quite good lama who has realization of the nature of mind and is close to the first level of bodhisattva. That's what we're talking about.

Q: At that level a person has complete choice.

A: Yes. Complete choice. Over one life.

Q: Just one?

A: Just one. If you are first-level bodhisattva, then one hundred.

Q: They can choose the time and birth and circumstances?

A: Definitely.

Q: And they choose their parents?

A: Yes. Choose their parents.

Q: Are the parents people they've known in their past life?

A: Maybe. Maybe not.

Q: Are the parents of a tulku special?

A: Right parents. "Right parents" for a tulku means they should be quite right [laughs]. They should be quite all right.

Q: When a tulku is reborn, what is the force that motivates them? What makes them will to be reborn?

A: Bodhichitta [the mind of awakening]: to help others, other beings. Otherwise why do you want to be around here? And have to eat three times a day! [Laughs.] And shave one time a day! [Laughs.] Sleep every day, go to bed every day. A lot of work! [Laughs.] Plus you get into unnecessary complications! [Laughs.]

Q: Does a tulku take rebirth with a specific project in mind, or does he think, "Whatever I can do for others, I will"?

A: Well, it depends. If a tulku is an old line of tulku then naturally his responsibility gets built up. But if it is a new tulku then maybe the responsibility could be more open. But if it is the third incarnation or the fourth incarnation or something like that, there is some responsibility built up around it. So that the fixed responsibility is maybe more than any open one, because you must spend time on what you are supposed to do instead of what you want to do. What you want to do becomes convenient and available for you after you complete your priorities, what you *should* do. If your previous incarnation built ten monasteries, your next life will have to take care of those ten before building another one. If that continues, by your tenth incarnation you might have two hundred monasteries to take care of. Plus people, plus so many things. That occupies your whole life.

In the incarnation system of Tibetan Buddhism, that one person who is reincarnated is given the same name. It's a title; it's a responsibility. It doesn't have to be that way, but it's become that way in Tibetan Buddhism.

Q: So the first one has perhaps meditated very much and attained some realization.

A: Yes! Yes!

Q: And the second, third, and fourth become more involved in administration?

A: No, no, no. A continuation. A continuation of the first one's work.

Q: And a continuation of the first one's meditation?

A: Meditation...umm...meditation is there. Whatever was attained is there, of course, but if the next incarnation will continue it or not also depends upon the circumstances, decisions, and the level of realization. But I would suggest, "Good to continue!" [Laughs.] Otherwise you might become rusty, yeah? A good sword has to be sharpened all the time. And cleaned.

Q: After a tulku is born, how much is *there* in his or her mind?

A: It depends on the level of realization. If the realization is very high, like first level bodhisattva, then everything is there. But if the level of realization is not quite that much, if it is below forbearance — heat, peak, forbearance [stages of the path] — before the first level of bodhisattva, if it is below forbearance, then it can even decline!

Q: But even good or high lamas, such as the Dalai Lama, Karmapa, or yourself....

A: Don't talk about me. Others, others.

Q: OK. Must they still study, meditate, learn again?

A: They should study, they should meditate because birth and death have a tremendous amount of impact as far as physical application is concerned. Their mind, the level of their mind, may be perfect, but with that [new] body, they have to learn how to talk, how to interpret letters, figures, and these things. That's a huge thing, but it might take a shorter time if they were familiar with them in their past.

But we cannot lock them into this one fixed situation, because everything might be perfect but they intentionally try to manifest something not so perfect in order to make some benefit out of it. That could be.

Q: Benefit for whom?

A: For the others. That also could be. When we offer lamps to the Buddha, we say, "You don't need a light to see things, but because we need to see things more clearly, we offer the lamp to your eyes." It could be that way.

Q: I feel I should mention another idea which might be wrong but which some people in the West believe: some people think that some tulkus are actual tulkus and some are sort of blessed. For example, a child is born in the right circumstances so the mind of the tulku blesses the child, but it's not really the tulku himself.

A: Then we cannot call it "tulku." We should call it "blessed," "chosen one" [laughs], or "blessed one."

Q: When we met Kalu Rinpoché or Karmapa, it was during their last life, when they were already older men. That they were tulkus or not tulkus didn't mean anything to us. It was simply the quality of who they were. It didn't matter how many certificates they had on the wall. It was just who they were. Now they're being reborn and it's not something —

A: It's a new thing. You haven't met one person in a different disguise [laughs].

Q: When you see these little persons in different disguises, are they the same for you?

A: Of course, of course, of course!

Q: One hundred percent?

A: Yes, one hundred percent. A tulku is one thing, but even when we see a fly, this has a past life and in the next life it may be a human being. That is there. There's nothing confused about it.

Q: Umdzé Zopa [master of ritual at Tai Situpa's main monastery in Sichuan Province, China] said when he met you, he kept on being afraid of you, completely terrified, because [the last Tai Situpa] Péma Wongchuk Gyalpo was a very wrathful person. Although he knew you were a very kind, gentle person, he was completely terrified of you. So the disguise has shifted and it seems like a new disguise.

A: I don't know. That's his problem! [Laughs.]

Q: So something changes. What stays the same?

A: The mind stays the same. And thought ... maybe stays the same. Reactions may be different [laughs].

RECOGNITION AND CONFIRMATION OF REINCARNATE LAMAS

Q: One of your responsibilities, perhaps one of the heaviest responsibilities you have, is to recognize or find the reincarnations of people's teachers. People come to see you to find their teachers.

A: Um, well...that's part of it. Part of it. Of course that's a big responsibility. But they could go to other great masters like Karmapa, His Holiness the Dalai Lama, His Holiness Sakya Trizin, Mindrol Ling Trichen, etc. They can also go to other Rinpochés. They don't have to come to me only. So that way I cannot say, "It's *my* big responsibility."

Q: Within the Kagyu tradition for some time, hasn't it been your responsibility?

A: It has been. It has been that way, yes, but that's how it has *been*. It could *be* the other way 'round. They could go to other great masters.

Q: What is the qualification necessary? There are only some — very few — masters to whom Tibetans would go to find their masters.

A: I think it's very much their faith and trust. That's very important. If they don't have faith and trust — you can see what's happened in the case of His Holiness Karmapa. You can see. Karmapa was born there [in eastern Tibet]; he was recognized through his own writing in the most historical, most traditional way, His Holiness the Dalai Lama was the supreme authority [who gave confirmation to the recognition], and he's already been enthroned in Tsurpu [Karmapa's main monastery in central Tibet] for more than one year. Still, some people don't want to believe. So if there's no faith, no trust, no devotion, it doesn't work for them. They might have some faith and trust, but if their ego is bigger than their faith, if their ego is bigger than their trust, if their ego is bigger than their devotion and compassion, then it doesn't work. They might have some, but...if the cloud is thicker than the sunlight, the sunlight cannot come through.

Q: So basically, if my teacher died I could go to anyone I had faith and trust in and ask him or her to find my teacher's reincarnation.

A: Yes. Can. Can. Can. Can. Of course, can. But traditionally, sometimes that could be appropriate, sometimes inappropriate. But in principle, you can. In principle.

Q: Have the Tai Situpas always had people come to them to find reincarnations of their teachers?

A: I think so. I think so. Sometimes more, sometimes less. But for that you'd have to look into history.

Q: How many tulkus have you recognized?

A: [Laughs] Just a few.

Q: I've heard that you've recognized over a hundred.

A: I don't know. A hundred is a lot of tulkus [laughs]. A big number!

Q: Only Kagyu masters?

A: Some Nyingma, some Gelug, some Sakya. But mainly Kagyu, Kam-tsang Kagyu. Also some Bonpo.

Q: Is this something you learned how to do? Did Karmapa teach you how to do it?

A: Karmapa taught me how to do it, of course. But "learning" — I don't know how to say it — perhaps we should say more like a transmission, I think, to describe [the process]. It's not so much learning. It's like when you're introduced to the nature of mind. Would you call it learning? A little bit. But it's more a transmission, isn't it? That way, more that way.

Q: If someone comes to you and says, "Please, my teacher has died: please find him!" what do you do?

A: If they say, "Find him," I'd say, "How do you know? How do you know where he is? Tell me where he is and I'll find him" [laughs]. It's not like that. They will come with total openness toward whether he is reborn or not. They are willing to accept if he is reborn or if he is not reborn. They are not coming with one idea that they want me to find him. And then I do my best, and sometimes it works and sometimes it doesn't work. Sometimes very clear, sometimes not very clear, but often I seek advice from greater masters for confirmation, such as His Holiness the Dalai Lama.

Q: Sometimes you don't ask for confirmation?

A: Sometimes I don't, when it is one hundred percent certain.

Q: When you say you do your best, what do you do?

A: Well, I try to use everything I know to locate [the reincarnation] and get all the indications.

Q: Does it depend on you, or does it depend on the person who has died?

A: Well, definitely the person who has died: that is the number one thing. If he is not around, then we cannot find him. So that's number one: that person. Number two is the faith and trust of the people who ask. Number three is my state of mind. If I'm awfully busy or having too many things to do, or like now, having so many unnecessary things cooked up by vested interest groups [laughs], then I don't think I can contemplate or meditate or really be clear. It's very difficult.

Q: Does it ever happen spontaneously that you find someone without trying?

A: I don't think so. I don't think so. Not up to now. It's possible, it's possible. But usually someone asks and then I start.

Q: If you've had a connection with this teacher in your life already, does it make it easier for you?

A: [Long pause.] I can't say. Some teachers...I had a very clear indication, like a personal indication from them, so maybe. I think all of them [in those cases] I had been very close to. So actually it could be possible. I've never thought about it like that.

Q: Do you have complete control over this process? For example, in the case of the Nechung Oracle [state oracle of Tibet], there is something completely outside of him that comes into him so he is able to see. How is it for you?

A: It's very difficult to describe that. I can't be accurate. I *think*, I *think* I have control over it, if I'm in a controllable condition [laughs]. Sometimes it works; otherwise, some tulkus they asked me [to say] ten years ago where they are, I don't know, even now. And then they went to some other teacher, and he found them already [laughs].

Q: Why?

A: I don't know.

Q: Is this work of recognizing reincarnations tiring for you or inspiring for you?

A: No, it's not tiring. I like the...clarity. It makes me feel very good and gets rid of all my — if I use ordinary language — stress and defilements, temporarily. I don't think I can ever get fed up with it. It's very nice. It is like a true thing: if you want to see the stars, the sky has to be clear, isn't it? With a cloudy sky you cannot see the stars. Look at the sky! [Points at the now heavily clouded sky.] Even the sun you cannot see! [Laughs.]

Q: What information do you give concerning the rebirth of a master?

A: It depends, it depends. What information I get, that's what I give. Sometimes the tulku is not born yet but the parents and everything become very clear so when he is born, I give that. Sometimes it has happened already: I give that. Sometimes it's just symbolic, very abstract: I give that. I have no choice! [Laughs.]

Q: Is this visual or aural information?

A: Could be anything.

Q: In your meditation, in a dream?

A: In dreams very little. Dreams are not very... how do you say?... Dreams could be used as some kind of way to get there, or some kind of reconfirmation, or sign. Dreams are only that, as far as I'm concerned.

Q: Do you then give the information to someone?

A: To whomever is asking. They have to do the work.

Q: Is the child then brought before you?

A: No, usually not. Most of the time they give me the details of the finding, then I check again. Sometimes they find quite a few — two or three possibilities — then I check again. Sometimes they have only one, sometimes two or three, four. Because [the circumstances of the birth are] very, very similar. Everything. But sometimes I also think that some people just make up some other [candidates] to test me. That's also possible.

Q: If there are a number of possibilities, how do they decide?

A: I do the same thing. I do it all over again.

Q: Do you ever have to test the child?

A: That's Hollywood! [Laughs.] I mean, even in one lifetime if you haven't seen somebody for years and they have put on weight or lost weight, can you recognize them? Very difficult, very difficult, even in one life. That person [the infant reincarnate master] went through a lot with death and rebirth. Quite a bit and still that person is a child [so he or she can't be expected to be tested].

Q: Sometimes people think a certain child is very special: the child must be a reincarnate lama.

A: Yes, a lot of that comes to us.

Q: If people feel this very strongly, what do you do?

A: It's very difficult. I have to give up on those because so many concepts are there. We can see so many concepts are there, so nothing can be done. It becomes very clouded. It cannot work.

Q: So if somebody feels this, he or she should give up.

A: That I don't know.

Q: What should a person do if he or she feels a child is a reincarnate master?

A: I don't know. Some lamas seem to be able to recognize them. I almost have never managed [to do so]. I cannot.

Q: Seems to be very common.

A: These days, these days.

Q: This didn't happen before?

A: I don't think so. In Tibet that didn't happen before. It would become like somebody saying, "My child is so bright, [he or she] should be the American president." They wouldn't say this in the old days. But nowadays Tibet has become very much like any other place.

Q: So before when there were a few candidates, this wasn't because the parents were pushing?

A: No, I don't think so. If parents are pushing a different candidate, that candidate is out naturally. Maybe in their mind they are hoping, but they cannot say so, and they really cannot do [anything to promote their child].

Q: Sometimes in the West, some people say of themselves, "I am a reincarnate master. I am a tulku."

A: Yes, well... That could be. I've also met quite a few of them [laughs].

Q: Is this generally confusion?

A: Well... could be either way. It could be true, but if they are, then somebody could have recognized them at the right time, not at the wrong time. They've already grown up, they have many complexes, and they think they're something. Everybody has doubts [in them], and it all becomes strange. I don't think that is necessary.

Q: In other forms of Buddhism in the world — in Sri Lanka, Thailand, Japan, or Korea — they don't have tulkus. Why did this become part of the Tibetan system?

A: Well, I don't know. That's the fact: I don't know the reason, to be honest. Maybe it didn't become practiced by them as a tradition, as a practice. It doesn't mean they don't know [who is a reincarnate master]. I think they know but it wasn't the system there, which was more the abbot system.

Q: These days most tulkus are born in Tibetan families and situations: do you expect that to change?

A: Tulkus will not be born in a place where it will be difficult and will not work. So they will be born only where it will work, where they will benefit others. So if there are obstacles, they have to be very meaningful, so they make that choice. It could change. I really don't know.

Q: There are very few women recognized as tulkus in the Tibetan system: will this change?

A: Well, it should be beneficial, it should be beneficial. There should be no obstacle. If there is an obstacle, it should be very meaningful. So maybe society will make it possible.

Q: One of the things you've done in your life so far is to preserve or to try to preserve Tibetan Buddhist traditions.

A: Try. Try. I will keep on trying until the end of my life, but it doesn't mean it will make a very big difference. But if I add a drop in the ocean, it's very good.

Q: Your lifework has been to preserve the tradition: how do you feel about it? Is the system working? How do you feel about its present and future?

A: Time is just the same. In ancient days, a day had just twenty-four hours; these days there are just twenty-four hours. In ancient times, people had five defilements [anger, desire, stupidity, jealousy, pride]; these days they also have the same ones. Truth is always the same. There's no change. So I think things may become a little bit different — it's natural to have some change but the principle shouldn't change. I mean, we shouldn't change for the sake of changing something. We shouldn't change because we're afraid we're going to be unpopular [laughs], or we want to be popular and that's why we change. I don't think so. There's no such thing as "modern" truth and "ancient" truth.

PART TWO

The Enthronement of a Reincarnate Master

The Celebration of the Opening of
One Hundred Doors
to Great Wonder

by
Jamgon Kongtrul Lodrö Tayé

Introduction to the Text

THE HISTORICAL CONTEXT

In 1700 a child was born in the tiny village of Alo Paljor, located a long day's journey from Dergé, one of the main cities of the eastern Tibetan region of Kham. The child was recognized as the eighth reincarnation of the Tai Situpa, one of the main lamas of the Oral Instruction Lineage (Kagyu) of Tibetan Buddhism. While some reincarnate lamas are like Hollywood sequels — they capitalize on the name of their predecessor but pale in comparison — this child grew to become one of the most outstanding of the Tai Situ incarnation line. He became renowned as a scholar, meditator, teacher, writer, administrator, and as the founder of a large monastery near his hometown which became his headquarters and the main residence of all subsequent Tai Situ Rinpochés. His name was Chökyi Jungné (Source of Spiritual Instructions); the monastery became known as Palpung (Mound of Glory).

A community of both monks and lay persons flourished around Palpung Monastery. Some of Chökyi Jungné's foremost disciples, also reincarnate masters, followed their master and made the monastery their principal residence; after his death, a thriving community welcomed the return of his reincarnation.

The new Tai Situpa, the ninth, Péma Nyinjé Wongpo (Lotus, Powerful Sun), did not equal his former lifetime's range of talents but he earned sincere respect far and wide for his mastery of the heart of the Buddha's teaching — meditation. He became the principal disciple of the thirteenth Karmapa, head of the Oral Instruction Lineage, was entrusted with the leadership of the lineage at Karmapa's death, and served as the principal instructor of Karmapa's reincarnation. Karmapa was the most illustrious among the great circle of masters who flocked to the ninth Tai Situpa for instruction. Another monk, who is now remembered as one of the greatest masters of the nineteenth century and among the most significant writers Tibet ever produced, came to Palpung Monastery in 1833 at the age of twenty, became Péma Nyinjé Wongpo's student, and always considered Tai Situ's inspiration, instruction, and influence the source of his spiritual life. That monk was Jamgon Kongtrul, the author of the following text.

Jamgon Kongtrul's devotion to Tai Situpa made him choose Palpung Monastery as his home. He founded a small retreat center at about a mile's distance from the main monastery, not far from a larger hillside meditation center where Péma Nyinjé Wongpo passed the last nineteen years of his life in retreat. Kongtrul spent most of his adult life at his meditation place, immersed in meditation, writing, and teaching. One of his uncharacteristic long journeys was made to central Tibet in 1857-58 to retrieve the new reincarnation of Tai Situpa, the tenth — Péma Kunzang (Lotus, Ever-Excellent).

Kongtrul records having first heard of Tai Situpa's reincarnation during the fourth lunar month of 1856:

> I heard the pleasant news that the supreme reincarnation of the Lord of Refuge has been reborn near Lake Nam-Tso, was recognized by the precious powerful victor [Karmapa] and invited to Tsurpu Monastery. (*The Autobiography of Jamgon Kongtrul*, 91b.2-3)

Later, Kongtrul himself was asked to travel to central Tibet as Palpung Monastery's representative to accompany the tulku on his return home. Since Kongtrul had never visited central Tibet, he first consulted with Jamyang Kyentsé Wongpo, his mentor and friend, on how he should prepare for his journey and what pilgrimage places to visit en route. The dates of Kongtrul's travel remind us that he lived in a day and age far removed from our own: in modern times, an unhurried trip from Dergé in Kham (eastern Tibet) to Lhasa might take up to a week by truck or jeep. Kongtrul left Palpung (near Dergé) on the twenty-second day of the sixth lunar month, 1857, and arrived at Tsurphu, Karmapa's monastery near Lhasa, three and a half months later, on the second day of the tenth month. There was also a different cadence to life in those times. Although he had made a journey halfway across the world (by the standards of his day), Kongtrul waited five days at the monastery before meeting the reason for his travel — the new Tai Situpa — since the seventh day was favored by "extremely good planets and stars." Further, Kongtrul took the opportunity of this unique sojourn in central Tibet to visit the major pilgrimage places Kyentsé had advised him to see: he arrived back home at Palpung, safe and sound with his young charge, on the tenth day of the tenth lunar month of 1858, more than fifteen months after his departure.

As mentioned below in the text, the enthronement of the new Tai Situpa took place on the fifth day of the first lunar month of 1859. Kongtrul wrote the text to prepare the Palpung community for the ceremony which marked the inauguration of their leader. Kongtrul was addressing a family reunion — the gathering of the Kagyu tribe in the presence of its chief, Karmapa; at its number two monastery, its headquarters in eastern Tibet, Palpung Monastery; on the occasion of the enthronement of the second-highest Kagyu hierarch, the Tai Situpa, a child then five years old. During the course of the event, probably close to the start, Kongtrul read the following text aloud to the assembly. As Kongtrul mentions in his book, his speech was followed by teaching given by three eminent scholars. In his *Autobiography*, his humility leads him to mention the others' teaching first:

[During the enthronement,] lamas and spiritual guides who are knowledgeable in Buddhist traditions explained the root texts of the Discourses and Tantras and I read the extensive explanation of *mandala* offerings. (*page 97a.1-2*)

Taken together, Kongtrul's keynote address and the lectures by these scholars constituted a statement of purpose for the Oral Instruction Lineage. Kongtrul recounted the history of the relationship of the two main leaders of the lineage — the Karmapa and Tai Situpa — and explained at length the vital importance of the spiritual master and of offerings to him, themes dear to Marpa and Milarepa's spiritual heirs. The lectures that followed his talk added to this verbal recollection of the common history, purpose, and path of Karmapa's lineage. The three scholars described the content of six important texts — three central to all Buddhists, and three vitally important to the Oral Instruction Lineage. Elsewhere, Kongtrul explained the particular relevance of these latter three to meditators of this tradition:

Since all [the leaders of the various branches of the Kagyu lineage] were exclusively holders of Milarepa's lineage of meditation practice, they did not delve deeply into the study and teaching of [the way of] characteristics [i.e., basic Buddhist theory grounded in the Lesser and Great Ways], but engaged only in the energetic practice of meditation. [Thus, the third Karmapa, Rangjung Dorjé, felt that] the three texts [*The Profound Inner Meaning, The Two Chapters*, and *The Highest Continuity*] were both sufficient and indispensable to develop the certitude born of study and reflection [which must precede] the practice of meditation.

[First,] *The Profound Inner Meaning*, in its eleven chapters, presents a general commentary on the entire range of tantras; and an extensive explanation of outer, inner, and "other" levels; particularly of the [body's] channels, energy winds, and vital essence. It is wrong for those who meditate on the Six Doctrines [of Naropa] to not know this text. [Second,] *The Two Chapters* contains the unbroken transmission of profound instructions produced by the genius of the king of the unsurpassable mother tantras, Lord Marpa.

It is extremely important for those who meditate on the creation and completion phases to know this text from the outset [of their practice]. [Third,] on the subject of *The Highest Continuity*, Lord Gampopa states: "The source text for our instructions in Great Seal [Mahamudra] is *The Highest Continuity*, a treatise of the Great Way [Mahayana], by the Honored One, Maitreya [Loving-Kindness]." In keeping with this teaching, Déshek Pagmo Drupa, Jikten Sumgon, and other masters continued to follow that school of thought. Further, the self-arisen victor [Rangjung Dorjé] and the others in the series of omniscient ones [the Karmapas] have consistently made the philosophy of this text the core [of their instructions]. Thus, for those who meditate on Great Seal, knowledge of this text is vitally important.

Therefore, these three texts do not consist of teachings of verbal explanation or of subjects for debate but are instructions in meditation practice and deep application. It is vitally important that the stream of these instructions be preserved undiminished by those who uphold the practice lineage. (*The Encyclopedia of Buddhism* 1: 505-506)

Thus, the enthronement ceremony provided an opportunity for all attending to remember the historical and spiritual roots of their common lineage.

This return and enthronement of the leader of the community — the spiritual master of many masters, the heart of many persons' lives — also presented an occasion for all the pomp and celebration Tibet was capable of. The current Tai Situpa likens an enthronement to the inauguration of an American president, "You know, with the horns and the American flags and things." For most Tibetans, the enthronement of their spiritual (and often political) leader was a once-in-a-lifetime event, and they made the most of it. The Tibetan community would know to wear their best brocades, the men decked with three knives (one of which would be a long sword), the women laden with their most ornate jewelry. Tibetans also have developed over the centuries ingenious, elaborate offerings, in the same way as Western Christians share collective knowledge of festive Christmas decorations. For example, large sacks of grain piled in offering at the foot of the throne are covered with outer cloth in a variety of brilliant colors; other offerings are festooned with decorative flourishes and arrayed on a sea of lush brocade. Long and noisy processions of lamas and monks carry all manner of silk banners and parasols and wear their ceremonial finest, including outrageous hats. They wade into the midst of this festival to the drone of horns, the beating of drums, and the crashing of cymbals. On an elevated throne, the Tibetan version of a pulpit, "borne" by eight lions sculpted around its base (hence a "lion throne"), they place an infant (often three to five years old), to be installed as the new chief of the monastery, the surrounding community, and often many other, smaller related monasteries and communities.

The setting of Tibetans' sometimes boisterous and chaotic "religious" ceremonies has little in common with the staid and solemn rituals of many other religions. In fact, Tibetan masters have remarked that what Western religions consider a correct attitude — the veil of solemnity that one dons on entering a church or temple — is, for Buddhists, nothing but a veil that must be removed. Tibetan Buddhist teaching stresses the natural state of mind: Tibetans might sit still for hours in deep meditation, in devotional group prayer, or in rapt, respectful attention to a lecture, but if they remain true to their culture's habits or the Buddhist teachings, the demons of artificial states, such as solemnity, do not trouble their minds. For many Westerners, however, an artificially solemn state is almost reflexive in "religious" settings and activities.

The momentous atmosphere of an enthronement is reflected in the style of this text: Kongtrul pulls out all the stops to impress upon his readers the importance of this teacher and this event. Those familiar with the Kongtrul's usual style — succinct, spare, intimate, precise, powerful — will not find those trademarks in his prose here. His use of words in this book creates an atmosphere of abundance: his vision of an enthronement is opulent, elaborate, extravagant, and grand. Kongtrul likens it to the appearance of the Buddha or a universal monarch in the world. This is perhaps the style reserved in other languages for the coronation of kings and queens. Thus his style in this book is not modern, nor was it even current in his own time — for example, he never once uses the common, colloquial word for *enthronement* in Tibetan (*khri bton*, pronounced *tree-tun*) but instead uses such grand terms in high honorific language as "investiture of authority" or "renewal of investiture of authority." He employed unusual flourishes and ornate constructions to make his Tibetan audience (and now us) take special note: this was no ordinary occasion.

Despite the fact that this text was written for a specific event that took place in 1859, this same event has been repeated hundreds, even thousands, of times since that day. Despite the fact that Kongtrul has written for a monastery led by Tai Situpa, who followed a tradition led by Karmapa, the devotion he expresses toward both is echoed by countless Tibetan communities, each praising its own spiritual leaders. Thus the content and the style of this book allow the reader to understand what the return of a spiritual master and his enthronement mean to every Tibetan Buddhist community. We examine one community's memory of its past spiritual leaders; we learn the steps they take to renew a vital part of their life — the acceptance of a new guide; and we hear their aspirations for the future as they join in prayer for the child who will lead their children and grandchildren. With a little imagination this exercise helps us see through the eyes and feel with the hearts of communities of Tibetan Buddhists of centuries past and of the present day.

A BRIEF OVERVIEW OF THE TEXT

The grand title of this text, *The Celebration of the Opening of One Hundred Doors to Great Wonder*, is surpassed by its subtitle, *A Complete Description of the Offering of the Universe to the Supreme Manifestation of Enlightenment, Our Loving Protector Tai Situpa, on the Occasion of His Assumption of the Lion Throne.* These titles indicate the content of the work and certainly set the tone: an enthronement of a reincarnate master is the opportunity for a celebration on an extravagant scale and for expressions of thanksgiving and devotion with sumptuous offerings.

Kongtrul divides his book into three chapters. Chapter One describes the five magnificent aspects of the manifestation of enlightenment in the world: the spiritual teacher, the location, the time, the entourage of persons around him or her, and the spiritual instructions. These five can be applied to describe the life of any great master; here Kongtrul uses this framework to introduce us to Tai Situ Rinpoché. In his case, the magnificent teacher is Karmapa; the magnificent setting, Palpung Monastery; the magnificent time, the auspicious timing of the enthronement; the magnificent entourage, Tai Situpa's circle of close disciples; and the magnificent spiritual instructions, the young reincarnate master's life in the world, which, Kongtrul informs us, represents a natural expression of awakened mind.

Chapter Two describes the lives of Tai Situ Rinpoché: Kongtrul explains how Tai Situpa's activity as a bodhisattva dedicated to the welfare of others has manifested throughout time and space. We read of Tai Situpa's lives in the heavens and on Earth, in India, Tibet, and China. Kongtrul shows how this teacher's activity through many lifetimes is woven into the fabric of Buddhist history — as the bodhisattva Loving-Kindness (Maitreya), disciple and regent of the Buddha Shakyamuni; as various tantric sages in India; as meditation masters who made important contributions to the spread and continuity of Buddhism in Tibet; and even as an emperor of China. Kongtrul provides a few details of each of the lives of the masters known as the Tai Situpas and makes sure the reader is made aware that Tai Situpa's enlightening presence in the world will culminate in his appearance as the next historical buddha, Buddha Maitreya, the successor to Buddha Shakyamuni.

Although this section focuses on Tai Situ Rinpoché, this kind of description, which situates a master's series of lifetimes within the sweep of Buddhist history, is a common feature of Tibetan hagiographies. It seems to have been important to many Tibetans to prove their master had repeatedly made significant contributions to Buddhism and had been either the master or disciple of other great masters during past centuries.

Kongtrul concludes this section with the statement that the return of the reincarnation of Tai Situpa should be accorded the same significance as "the appearance of the Buddha in the world," and he includes many quotations from the Buddha's discourses and tantras which laud the spiritual master as the Buddha incarnate. This is not entirely hyperbole. Although the title Living Buddha was given to the reincarnate lamas by the Chinese rather than the Tibetans, the Tibetan word *tulku* — enlightenment manifest physically in the world — has much the same connotation. For devout disciples of these masters, these were not empty titles. Kongtrul and other meditators regarded their spiritual masters with the same respect they would have shown the Buddha.

Chapter Three introduces us to an enthronement ceremony: this consists of the presentation of offering upon offering, indicating thanks from the former disciples to the master for his return, best wishes from other masters, and the continued faith of all. According to Kongtrul, the centerpiece of the offerings consists of the offering of the universe in the form of what is called a *mandala*. This consists of the imagined offering of the Buddhist conception of the universe filled to overflowing with all that is pleasing from the worlds of gods and human beings. These gifts are mentally multiplied to infinity and presented to the child reincarnate master in the form of piles of rice on a gold or silver circular disc, arranged in time with the words of the mandala offering prayer the assembly sings in unison. Kongtrul considers this to be the most important offering made at the enthronement ceremony: he describes in detail its origins, meaning, and content. (In another one of Kongtrul's works in English, *The Torch of Certainty*, he devotes a chapter to this offering, one of the four practices done in preparation for tantric meditation.)

The mandala offering is based upon the Buddhist conception of the world and universe. That it in no way resembles our modern concepts does not seem to be disconcerting to Buddhist teachers. As the current Tai Situpa has remarked, "The Buddha didn't come into the world to teach geography." Accuracy aside, this world is imagined to be both elegant and elaborate, filled with every source of majesty and pleasure. This is the world in party dress, a welcome relief from some conventional Buddhist pictures of the universe as a dark and fearful place.

The Celebration of the Opening of
One Hundred Doors
to Great Wonder

A Complete Description of the Offering of the Universe
to the Supreme Manifestation of Enlightenment,
Our Loving Protector, Tai Situpa,
on the Occasion of
His Assumption of the Lion Throne

by

Jamgon Kongtrul Lodrö Tayé

The Celebration of the Opening of One Hundred Doors to Great Wonder

Om. May excellent virtue prevail!

The splendid qualities of life
And of the peace beyond,
In aspects wholly positive
Yours, like Ganges' sands, abound.
The moment I remember you,
And your lotus feet recall,
Like wishing on a magic gem —
My wishes granted, one and all.
Illustrious master Karmapa,
Three Jewels in one form living now,
To you and all your spiritual heirs:
At your feet I humbly bow.

Your glorious dawn of power, wealth,
And well-being here has come.
The acts which are its single source
Extend your city's wide dominion:
The world is covered by your sun —
Canopy of Buddha's doctrine pure —
For those who seek for wisdom, shine!
Never set; life's virtues thus ensure.

This drink of nectar — homage rendered to Karmapa, our supreme, highest source of refuge, and verses intended to create excellent virtue — indicates the subject of this speech. At this time, the supreme manifestation of the perfect marks and signs of enlightenment in a physical configuration, the omniscient Loving Protector, Karma Tai Situ, has blossomed anew. We thank him for his kindness in fearlessly reassuming his place on the great throne of spiritual instruction which is triumphant in every domain. Further, we request that his three secret spheres [body, speech, and mind] remain steadfast as indestructible phenomena, and we encourage him to continually turn the wheel of profound and all-encompassing spiritual instructions. To give substance to our appreciation and requests, we offer a cloudlike mass of material gifts which, in being given, augment our merit and wisdom. These gifts begin with the full offering of the universe in the form of a mandala. This text, which provides a short description of this event, has three chapters: Chapter One provides an introductory explanation of the five magnificent aspects of Tai Situpa's manifestation in the world; the focus of Chapter Two, the main body of the text, explains the reasons why we make offerings to this individual; and Chapter Three presents a step-by-step description of the act of offering mandalas and thereby provides a definitive explanation of this kind of offering.

CHAPTER ONE

The Five Magnificent Aspects of Our Spiritual Master's Manifestation in the World

The tradition of the Great Way (Mahayana) and the tantras find their common source in the five magnificent aspects of manifest enlightenment. Similarly, the outstanding enlightened activity of the father Karmapa, lord of all the victorious ones, the noble bodhisattva Lotus-in-Hand (Padmapani) incarnate,[1] and his spiritual heirs originated with these five. These aspects of enlightenment create in our world all that brings happiness and well-being, as well as the precious doctrines of scripture and realization. Since the breadth of these abundant riches is pervasive and definitely continues to increase, we begin with a description of the way [our spiritual master, Tai Situpa] manifests these five magnificent aspects: (1) his teacher, (2) his residence, (3) the time of his enthronement, (4) his entourage, and (5) his spiritual instructions.

TAI SITUPA'S MAGNIFICENT TEACHER: KARMAPA

The Flower Ornament Discourse states:

> Though awakening's ocean they've fully attained,
> An ocean of others in darkness remain —
> To bring beings' minds to full maturation,
> They show an ocean of awakened intentions
> And constant great oceans of unclouded deeds:
> The Joyful Ones' manifestations are these!

Similarly, from the perspective of definite truth, our teacher, the sole refuge of the gods and all beings, the great omniscient mighty king [Karmapa] has, since beginningless time, been completely awakened within the perfect simplicity of the sphere of ultimate enlightenment. His form, which expresses the perfect splendor of enlightenment, possesses the five certainties,[2] which produce his forms and pure lands arranged in vast oceans of clouds. For as long as space exists, an inconceivable number of emanations diffuse from these forms to skillfully guide to authentic liberation within unsurpassable great awakening the infinite numbers of beings who have been overwhelmed by confusion. The great influence of such courage has united in his person all the enlightened activity of the buddhas and bodhisattvas; thus he is known as the mighty victor, the illustrious Karmapa. The single canopy of his name covers an ocean of pure realms; his form is inseparable from that of the protector of the Himalayan region, the bodhisattva All-Seeing One (Avalokiteshvara). At his exalted stage of awakening, his true life of freedom[3] is not concealed but is clearly revealed to all. He has thus become an impartial upholder of the Buddha's teaching and a refuge for all beings. He has been lauded as a Living Buddha by such mighty individuals as the great emperors [of China], rulers of the world who have received the mandate of heaven.[4] The series of his lives, a garland of jewels, has appeared uninterruptedly: the present Karmapa is his fourteenth incarnation. Because he will later demonstrate the attainment of enlightenment as the sixth historical buddha, named Lion, beings are protected from fearful rebirths in miserable existences and are reborn in pure lands by the effect of just having heard his name. In particular, they will be reborn in the circle of disciples of the sixth buddha, Lion. This has been repeatedly predicted in the infallible scriptures composed by the knower of the three times, the master from Oddiyana, Guru Rinpoché. This is not a case of an ordinary individual receiving undue praise: Karmapa is the primordial lord of all spiritual instructions; he is the sole father of all buddhas; and he has attained the rank of an unsurpassable teacher.

The omniscient, loving protector of beings, Tai Situpa, a precious supreme manifestation of enlightenment, is in essence inseparable from the victorious Karmapa, although he appears sometimes as Karmapa's spiritual master, sometimes as his disciple. His skillful compassion and authority allow him to assume self-reliant leadership of the vehicle of enlightened activity.

Not even a tiny fraction of this spiritual father and son's [Karmapa and Tai Situpa's] lives of freedom and outstanding qualities can be accurately seen or described by an ordinary feeble-minded individual like me. They do not even fall within the range of experience of those known to be the major gods of this world, such as Indra and Brahma, or even of those higher than they, the Listeners and the Solitary Sages.[5] *The Reunion of Father and Child Discourse* states:

> It may be possible to span
> Heaven's paths the birds' wings trace
> And even plumb the depths of seas,
> Calculating vase by vase;
> The grandest mountain might be weighed
> Were it on a balance placed,
> But Buddha's qualities' far bounds
> Exceed every mind's embrace.

Why are such great qualities not visible to persons such as we? *The Jewel Palm Discourse* states:

> No sun will blind men ever see,
> Its rise in every world concealed;

"It shines," the seeing will attest:
To each his own acts' fruits revealed.

In the same way, to see clearly and to comprehend the lives of freedom and the outstanding qualities of buddhas, bodhisattvas, and other spiritually advanced individuals, a level comparable to those exalted persons must be attained. Apart from persons who have reached such attainment, we ordinary beings are sinking in the ocean of our own confusion: those whose eyes of wisdom are covered by the cataracts of ignorance have no opportunity to see or to comprehend the life of freedom of higher individuals. As it is said:

The feeble faith of those who live
On life's common, mundane plane
Of Buddha's great awakening
Can no comprehension gain.

Therefore, these masters act with consummate skill in ways that are appropriate to our fortune in life: they manifest bodies comparable to the bodies of ordinary beings; their voices resonate in the patterns of ordinary speech; and their minds influence others in ways that are accessible to ordinary thought. Such manifestations in themselves constitute wondrous and particularly sublime compassion and enlightened activity, what we should accept as the heart of our faith and devotion.

In brief, the mighty victor, the great Karmapa, developed immeasurable compassion for the good of the people and the spiritual life of the Himalayan region and has repeatedly displayed incarnations which manifest the physical presence of enlightenment in the world. His conduct, triumphant in every domain, has created a great wave throughout the world of pervasive good, for Buddhism and for humanity in general. Following him, other schools have adopted many names and titles for their leaders, such as "reincarnate master" or "spiritual leader," and this wise custom [of recognition of such masters] has spread widely. In fact, however, other traditions have simply imitated the victorious Karmapa's example.[6]

These are not pretentious words: each of the series of reincarnations of this victorious spiritual father and son [Karmapa and Tai Situpa] has been openly and clearly predicted and their outstanding qualities lauded in the adamantine speech of the second Buddha, the precious master from Oddiyana, Guru Rinpoché. They have been installed as the glorious protectors of humanity and of Buddhism in the Himalayan region. Not only have their lives been foretold: their qualities and enlightened activity are clearly evident and are renowned throughout China and Tibet. Those who have temporal power, great influence and wealth, a great entourage of monks, or appear to be important persons in the world respect others of high [political or worldly] rank, but no one rivals the lives of freedom and the outstanding qualities of this spiritual father and son. Therefore, critical examination by logic or careful consideration by those endowed with impartial wisdom reveals that this spiritual father and son have, throughout the series of their lives, demonstrated the four miracles that lead others to enlightenment: physically, their great merit has led others to enlightenment; verbally, the variety of their instructions have led others to enlightenment; mentally, their clairvoyance has led others to enlightenment; and their inconceivable qualities and enlightened activity have led others to enlightenment. Since their mastery of these four miracles is comparable to that of the perfect Buddha, they are like second buddhas. The illuminating radiance from the pure body, speech, and mind of these two refuges and protectors of beings, like that of the sun and moon, fills the three regions of this world with beauty.[7]

TAI SITUPA'S MAGNIFICENT RESIDENCE: PALPUNG MONASTERY

Our world, the Land of Jambu, is comprised of twelve distinct regions, one of which is the Small Land of Jambu, the pure land where the thousand buddhas [of this eon] appear and turn the wheel of spiritual instruction. In particular within this land lies the region which the exalted bodhisattva Mighty All-Seeing One made the area of his enlightened influence, the Himalayan region, comprised of both Tibet and Greater Tibet. Within the province of Greater Tibet, the region that is unique from the point of view of size, wealth, and influence is known as the Six Mountain Ranges of Do-Kham [eastern Tibet], one of which is known as Drida Zalmo Range. Many erudite and accomplished masters, known throughout the Buddhist world as outstanding persons, lions among men, have come into the world in this area: such masters include Déshek Pagmo Drupa, Ka[tok] Dampa Déshek, the great accomplished Karma Pakshi, and the omniscient Tenpa Nyinjé. This is the region where the golden lineage of the great kings of Dergé, gods from the heaven of Brahma, have successively been of unrivaled service to the doctrine of the Buddha.

Within this region is found one of Do-Kham's twenty-five great areas of sacred ground. These places were consecrated by the glorious spiritual king from Oddiyana, Guru Rinpoché, as inseparable from the world's eternally existing major sacred sites. Of the twenty-five, this region's great area of sacred ground, called Vajra Chitta and Devi Kotra,[8] represents the heart of enlightened qualities. An ocean of awareness-holders, accomplished ones, and dakas and dakinis of the three places[9] gather like clouds on this mountain. It has numerous ornaments, such as treasures of jewels and spiritual instructions, and one hundred and eight signs of the presence of enlightened body, speech, and mind, and other naturally appearing indications of Buddhist influence. The protector of the palace of the bodhisattva Great Compassionate One, the virtuous *gényen* Vajra Blazing Glory (Dorjé Pal-bar),[10] resides in front of this place. To its right stands Tsadra Rinchen Drak, a cliff inseparable from the earthly pure land, glorious Charitra. The ten virtues of a region[11] and the excellent features of a piece of land as described by geomancy can all be found here. This place has been consecrated by many greatly advanced masters, embodiments of wisdom, and principally by the series of incarnations of the wearer of the dark-red crown, Tai Situpa. The temple here, surrounded by the joyful grove of the monastic community, resounds with the reverberation of the great drum of spiritual instructions. The monastery is known as Mound of Glory, the Place of the Wheel of Spiritual Instruction of the Doctrine of Shakyamuni (Palpung Toobten Chökor Ling), renowned throughout the Himalayan region.

THE MAGNIFICENT TIME: THE OCCASION OF THE INVESTITURE OF TAI SITUPA

According to the collection of the excellent speech of the Buddha, our teacher, the peerless Siddhartha, sat in the center of the great miracle temple at Sravasti [north-central India], surrounded by an oceanlike gathering of gods and other beings. In response to the requests of King Prasenajit and other disciples, the Buddha demonstrated ordinary and extraordinary great miracles for a period of fifteen days, surpassing all in the three worlds. These miracles totally defeated the followers of evil religions; the teachings of Buddha appeared brightly illumined throughout the three existences, like the moon shining in a cloudless sky.[12] This time is thus well known as an auspicious festival when the force of virtuous activity is greatly multiplied.

From the perspective of astrology, this occasion marks the beginning of a new year, the male iron monkey year. It was during the monkey year that the glorious master from Oddiyana, Padmasambhava, first appeared on a lotus in the center of a lake, his body displaying the indestructible marks and signs of perfection. Because of this and other special acts performed by this master during the monkey year, this time is blessed.

Of the two declinations, the circle of the seven horses[13] is in its north declination, on what is known as the day of the gods. This occasion is widely appreciated for its influence, which increases longevity, merit, wealth, power, talent, and fame. Of the four seasons, today's investiture takes place in the first spring month, the gateway to the summer monsoons which usher in every positive quality that nurtures all forms of life. Of the two phases of the moon, it takes place during the waxing phase, when all negativity dissipates and the configuration of auspicious virtue increasingly augments the positive. Of the days of the month, the event takes place on the morning of the first completion [the fifth day of the month], symbolic of the spontaneous complete fulfillment of all wishes. Concerning the planets, sun, moon, stars, conjunctions, and actions of astrology, the system of calculation of these five aspects based on the tantra of the glorious Wheel of Time (Kalachakra) predicts that everything will be extremely positive. According to calculation based on numerology, [the word] Tarkala and the result of calculation of astrological influences based on the great Chinese tradition [both] indicate that various negative influences will be kept at a very safe distance and many various harmonious influences will appear spontaneously.

THE MAGNIFICENT ENTOURAGE SURROUNDING TAI SITUPA

Tai Situpa's entourage resembles the demonstration of unique enlightened activity by buddhas and high bodhisattvas: he is surrounded by bodhisattvas and listeners who have clairvoyance and miraculous powers, awareness-holders and dakinis, an ocean of committed guardians and protectors of the instructions, powerful positive spirits, and others such as gods, nagas, *yakshas*, and semi-human spirits. These invisible beings delight in the Buddha's teaching and gather in all the available space above or on the ground around Tai Situpa, like a dense cluster of sprouting sesame seeds. They gaze in faith at the face of this master and drink the nectar of his words as spiritual instruction.

As for the members of his entourage who are visible to all, *The Discourse of the Symbol of Moving to Courage on the Crown of the Heads of All Buddhas* states:

> After my [the Buddha's] passing beyond suffering, the bodhisattvas and *arhants* will assume rebirth during degenerate times in a body of the same qualities as the disciples. These emanations in various forms will liberate those who dwell within cyclic existence.

In the manner foretold in this passage, many masters appear in Tai Situpa's entourage. For example, the precious master, Guru Chökyi Wongchuk [abbreviated below as Chöwong], the emanation of the ultimate fruition of the speech[14] of the Buddhist king Tsangpa Lha'i Métok [commonly known by the name King Trisong Dé-u Tsen], was the sovereign of all accomplished treasure revealers. His reincarnation, the nephew of Jangchub Dorjé [the ninth Karmapa] realized the identical nature of his own mind and appearing phenomena and was thereby able to perform such feats as leaving impressions of his hands and feet in solid stone. He was widely recognized as a powerful accomplished master and was considered to be the intentional rebirth of Lama Chöwong. Thus he is known as Chöwong Tulku.

Another master was proclaimed by Mikyö Dorjé [the eighth Karmapa] to be an emanation of his own enlightened activity. Known as either Dawkpo Go-nyon or the close attendant Karma Sidral, he fashioned the great statues of the male and female protectors used in the dances at Karmapa's main monastery, Ok-min Tsurpu, and showed expertise in the sculpting of all forms of statues. His reincarnation, known as the fully ordained monk Döndrup, pleased Dudul Dorjé [the thirteenth Karmapa] by both serving as his master and his attendant. His subsequent rebirth became known as Döndrup Tulku. These two teachers, Chöwong and Döndrup Tulkus, have now been reborn as the nephews and spiritual sons of Tegchok Dorjé [the fourteenth

Karmapa]. The qualities of their renunciation and realization are complete in every respect: they have become illustrious protectors of the Buddha's teaching and of beings.

Langdro Translator, Könchok Jungné was reincarnated as the great treasure revealer and the sovereign of spiritual life Ratna Lingpa. The manifestation of the ultimate fruition of his spiritual practice was his [later] rebirth as the great awareness holder Long-sal Nyingpo. This master promised to take rebirth intentionally to illuminate the doctrine of the practice [i.e., Kagyu] lineage. Accordingly, he has reappeared in three successive lifetimes [as the noble master Norbu Sampel and others], during which the influence of his service to the teaching of the precious practice lineage has been as significant as that of the father and main spiritual heirs of the lineage. His present incarnation, foretold by the second buddha, the master from Oddiyana, Guru Rinpoché, is named Karma Drubgyu Tenzin Trinlé Chok.

The noble spiritual master [Jamyang Kyentsé Wongpo?] has stated:

Da-ö Shunnu, Gunu Nata,
And he who gained the boon
Of longevity, Tang-tong Gyalpo,
Was as Jivadhyana known.

As stated, the master blessed by Dawkpo Da-ö Shunnu (Gampopa), Yutok Yonten Gonpo, the lord of accomplishment Tang-tong Gyalpo, and others was Kumarajiva, who reappeared in living form as the noble master Samten. His rebirth, the embodiment of wisdom, love, and capability, is the great reincarnate master, the noble spiritual teacher Karma Tegchok Tenpel. These two masters, Karma Drubgyu Tenzin and Karma Tegchok Tenpel, are known as the two Öntrul Rinpochés.

Another member of the entourage was the great elder Aniruddha, when he lived at the time of the Buddha; when he appeared in the presence of the master from Oddiyana, he was

Prince Mutri Tsenpo. He was later reborn as Rinchen Puntsok, spiritual leader of the Drigung Kagyu spiritual school, and has taken rebirth in a series of similarly pure lives. The last one was as the treasure revealer and awareness-holder known as Mingyur Dorjé Drakpo Nuden Tsal. His life of freedom, during which he accomplished clairvoyance, miracles, and other feats, is inconceivable. The fourth in the series of his reincarnations now numbers among Tai Situpa's entourage.

Another master was the great accomplished one Humkara in the holy land [India], and in Tibet was Köntön Lu-i Wongpo. As an emanation of these and other masters, he came into the world to bring peace to the minds of beings of the degenerate age, through a wondrous life of freedom which surpasses the imagination, known as the treasure revealer and awareness-holder Rolpé Dorjé Ta-dun Trin-dra Tayé Tsal. The fourth in the series of his reincarnations also numbers among Tai Situpa's entourage.

These exemplary individuals are those particularly noteworthy among a gathering made up exclusively of persons with a fortunate karmic connection to the Buddhist teaching. The outstanding supreme physical manifestations of enlightenment within Tai Situpa's entourage have intentionally taken rebirth in the world by the power of their aspirations, and they now accomplish great waves of benefit for Buddhism and for humanity. The members of his entourage's assembly of spiritual mentors have completed their study, reflection, and meditation for their own benefit and now serve others by maintaining the conduct of bodhisattvas through the four means of gathering disciples.[15] The ascetic lifestyle and great courage of the powerful yogis of his entourage has led them to turn their backs on the eight worldly concerns[16] and to follow the path of devotion and compassion to its destination: the attainment of a treasure vault of experience and realization. The superlative innate and developed wisdom and the diligence of the assembly of the supreme heirs, the learned of the entourage, has caused the mastery of their knowledge of the discourses, tantras, arts, and sciences to fully blossom. The great storehouse of their self-confidence has completely opened, and they now illuminate the doctrine of the Victorious One through teaching, debate, and writing. The assembled gathering of the genuinely learned, noble, and excellent virtuous [monastic] community within his entourage acts according to the conduct prescribed in the three Buddhist disciplines. Their minds are rich in the experience of the three trainings: they are truly worthy recipients of the lay community's respect. The lord of the region who belongs to this entourage — courageous, mighty, and of an expansive penetrating intellect — acts, along with his court, as the stable pillar of this spiritually inclined kingdom. Finally, the entourage is completed by male and female laypersons who are wealthy in faith and in material possessions, and who live together harmoniously united in the thought and the practice of virtue. In brief, like the full moon surrounded by the constellations, Tai Situpa is encircled by an oceanlike gathering of disciples who have single-minded devotion toward him.

THE MAGNIFICENT SPIRITUAL INSTRUCTIONS

"Spiritual instructions" refers to what is called *dharma* in Sanskrit. This word is derived from the root *drudrhia*, meaning "holding." It is translated into Tibetan as the word *chö* [spelled *chos*], a term that has ten meanings.[17] *Principles of Elucidation* states:

> *Dharma* means phenomena,
> Path, life span, merit, nirvana,
> Mind's image, objects, regulations,
> Sacred texts, and world religions.

In this context, the meaning among these that concerns us is *dharma* as outstanding authentic spiritual instructions. Its characteristics are described by the master Vasubandhu:

> Buddha the Teacher's authentic instructions
> Encompass both scripture and realization.

Authentic spiritual instructions are called this since their subject encompasses realization, including the truth of cessation, and the instructions contained in the pure scriptures of the Buddha. The instructions that express this subject, including the path of cessation, are found in the treatises written as commentaries to the words spoken by the Transcendent One by such masters as the six ornaments, who beautify this world by their presence, the two exemplary masters, the four great masters, the six gateways to erudition, the ten major pillars who supported the lineages of explanation of the tantras in the region of Tibet, and the originators of the major traditions of the eight great practice lineages of Tibet and their worthy followers.[18] Therefore these teachings are called authentic spiritual instructions. As it is said:

> The excellent speech of Buddha's word
> And great masters' commentaries —
> The Canon and the Treatises —
> Buddhist teachings' two categories.

> These collections in this world ensure
> Shakyamuni's doctrine will long endure.

Since this subject is so well known, it will not be dwelt upon here. The essence of authentic spiritual instructions can be described as follows:

> Genuine spiritual instructions
> Relieve all pain and obscurations.

As stated, anything which removes the sufferings of beings and provides an antidote to their obscurations has the nature of spiritual instruction. What is called "the wheel of spiritual realization" has been interpreted in a number of ways. The Detailed Exposition School considers that only the path of seeing qualifies as the wheel of spiritual realization. According to the Discourse School, three paths — of seeing, meditation, and no further learning — are the wheel of spiritual realization. Followers of the Great Way consider that the five paths — of accumulation, application, seeing, meditation, and no further learning — as well as the path of complete liberation belong to the wheel of spiritual realization.

Cycle or *wheel* is the equivalent of the Sanskrit word *chakra*, which can mean "to move," "to gather," "to sever," etc. In this context the word is used to indicate the movement of blessing to the minds of the disciples, the gathering of many forms of virtuous activity, and the means to sever the obscurations and obscuring emotions. *The Former Lives of the Buddha* states:

> Its innate nature: the moon's bliss
> Sun's light, fire's heat, wind's speed,
> And great ones' joy in compassion
> Which fosters altruistic deeds.

All physical, verbal, or mental deeds displayed by buddhas or spiritually advanced bodhisattvas act only as means to extinguish the sufferings of others and to remove their obscurations. Therefore, all their acts, be they physical, verbal, mental, or of their qualities or enlightened activity, constitute the spontaneous wheel of spiritual realization.

An example of this occurred in the heaven Joyous: the young god, holy White Crown-Ornament [Shakyamuni Buddha's name in his last life before his birth in this world], designated the bodhisattva Loving-Kindness [Maitreya] as he who would assume his seat on the lion-supported throne called Excellent Qualities within the great assembly hall known as Lofty Spiritual Instructions. He then placed a turban and a crown on the bodhisattva's head and empowered him as his regent. Thus the spontaneous great wheel of spiritual realization of the buddhas' lineage continued without interruption. In the same way, this bodhisattva, Loving-Kindness, in many of his series of lives has been empowered as the regent of the Buddha's spiritual instruction and given command of the chariot of enlightened activity. This auspicious connection has continued to the present day:[19] Karmapa, the sole father of all enlightened ones, the protector of the Himalayan region, the eminent supreme Lord of the World, in his continuous fearless expression of the symphony of the instructions of the Great Way, has given full investiture to Tai Situpa, the able son of the Buddha, the true form of the Protector Loving-Kindness, the spiritual master of the three worlds, on the lofty throne of spiritual instruction which is totally triumphant in every direction.

This sincere, sublime praise on the part of the Karmapa constitutes the first virtue [of Tai Situpa's magnificent spiritual instructions] which illuminates every part of the three regions. This original virtue leads to the subsequent virtue: Tai Situpa's renunciation within and study of the precious doctrine of both scripture and realization, which will surely reach, increase, and long endure within the highest stages of awakening. The force of this subsequent virtue will lead to the final virtue: the uplifting of the lives of all beings within the realms of existence and the creation of easy access for all to the ultimate glory, enlightenment. His activity will have an effect like the warmth of the summer in which the wealth of nature flourishes: his acts will naturally multiply all forms of excellence which augment positive qualities. This connection [between the original, subsequent, and the final virtues of his spiritual instruction] will increase the illumination of his amazing accomplishment.

This concludes the introductory remarks.

CHAPTER TWO

Tai Situpa's Special Qualities

I will now describe briefly Tai Situpa's special qualities in order to explain why offerings are made to this spiritual master.

A person worthy of veneration by all beings, including the gods, and an authentic source of refuge for them all, the omniscient Karma Tai Situ, has since the beginning of time attained full awakening within the sphere of totality and completed his activity. However, by the force of his pervasive compassion, he continually works for the welfare of beings whose numbers fill all space, for as long as life remains in the universe. *The Reunion of Father and Child Discourse* states:

> Great skillful spiritual hero
> For a hundred million years,
> You, the one victorious,
> As the Buddha did appear.
> To bring to full maturity
> All living things, you once again
> Will reveal yourself, our guide,
> As many ones enlightened.

As stated here, Tai Situpa works for the good of the world in a variety of manifestations according to the needs of others. In some realms, he demonstrates the attainment of full and perfect awakening; in some he appears as a bodhisattva or as a spiritual adept; in others, as a universal monarch;[1] as the gods Brahma or Vishnu; as a sun, a moon, or a radiant jewel; as medicine, a boat, or a bridge; or as any physical manifestations of enlightenment — as created forms, ordinary beings, or supreme buddhas — whose displays of forms to guide others are beneficial to all. In the future, during the age of perfection,[2] when the longevity of humans reaches 80,000 years, he will reach enlightenment as the fifth buddha of this Fortunate Eon,[3] the Transcendent One known as Protector Loving-Kindness. He will thereby prevent the interruption of the acts of buddhas in this world.

The Ornament of the Discourses states:

> On exemplary diligence
> The child of the Buddha does rely:
> Once work's begun for others' sake,
> The bodhisattva ever strives.
> A single act of virtue
> On perfections' course once set
> May take a million eons' time
> Yet never cause regret.

As stated, he will appear again in the world to serve others in infinite ways until cyclic existence becomes empty. In particular, he develops an even greater force of compassion and diligence toward worlds like our own, which is filled with the five signs of degeneration.[4] To liberate those beings who have no protection whatsoever, he dons the great armor of fearlessness; *The Ornament of the Discourses* states:

> Energetic for others' sake,
> The embodiment of compassion
> Caught in hell's unceasing pain,
> Other's good his sole intention,
> Feels toward that world of torment
> Not the slightest apprehension.

Tai Situpa really lives the meaning of these words. At the present time, he repeatedly takes rebirth within the phenomenal world, but these lives are not in the slightest way for his own benefit. *The Condensed Version of the Perfection of Wisdom Discourse* states:

> Great persons work to make realms pure,
> Bring others to maturity,
> Complete perfections, and serve mankind —
> Their life in its entirety.

As stated, Tai Situpa acts only for the good of others in purifying the realms of buddhas, bringing others to spiritual maturity, and in demonstrating the way to truly practice the six perfections. Therefore, his life of freedom remains solely within the domain of experience of enlightened ones. However, if we look back to examine how he is known to have appeared to those of limited vision, he appears[5] in the heaven Joyous as the Buddha's regent, Protector Loving-Kindness. In the pure land Blissful, he appears as the great bodhisattva Source of Spiritual Instruction and as an ocean of other manifestations of bodhisattvas on the pure stages of awakening[6] who fully purify the realms of the enlightened ones. In the land of the spiritually exalted [India], he appeared as the great master Dombipa; as the master who attained an indestructible body, Shri Singha; and as the immortal Darikapa and other masters who reached the stage of great accomplishment. While assuming this multitude of forms as meditation masters, he spread the teachings of the Vajra Way.

Further, he appeared in the region of Tibet during the original spread of Buddhism: as the Chinese master Jampal Sangwa (also known as the venerable Gyim Shang), he provided the original analysis of the geomancy of Samyé, Tibet's first monastery, through mastery of mantras and astrology. Further, as the bilingual Denma Tsémang, a helper to the translators, he was accepted as a disciple by the king of spiritual instructions from Oddiyana, Guru Rinpoché. Denma Tsémang became the chief recipient of the Wrathful Mantra deity meditation instructions and served as a scribe for many of the yellow parchment texts.[7] During the period of the later spread of Buddhism, Tai Situpa appeared as the spiritual heart-son of the eminent Naropa and Métripa, the deity Joyous Vajra (Hevajra) appearing in human form, known as Marpa the Translator from Lhotrak. Marpa is renowned throughout the Tibetan Himalayan region as the source of the river which became the ocean of accomplished masters of the Oral Instruction (Kagyu) Lineage. Thereafter Tai Situpa worked for the benefit of others in various manifestations, some appearing alone, some simultaneously with others. These included Pang Kenchen Özer Lama; the great noble one of Jonang, Taranata; and many other emanations as holy persons who were both learned and accomplished. All these masters spread Buddhism far and wide. In manifestations as major and minor kings, including Rabten Kunzang Pak, the Buddhist king of Gyantsé; and Ngawang Jikten Wongchuk of Rin-poong, he ruled vast areas according to Buddhist law.

In particular, Tai Situpa has intentionally taken rebirth in a series of lives in order to sustain the vitality of the inner doctrine of the practice lineage. As the nephew of Gampopa, he was the master known as Gompo Tsultrim Nyingpo, the main inheritor of the transmission of Great Seal (Mahamudra) realization from the incomparable doctor from Dawkpo [Gampopa]. As Drogön Réchen Sonam Drakpa, he was empowered as spiritual regent by the illustrious first Karmapa, Dusum Kyenpa. As Yeshé Ö, he served as the close attendant of the second Karmapa, Karma Pakshi, and was the first to open the gate of the sacred ground of the new Charitra.[8] As the greatly accomplished Ratna Bhadra of Ringo, he was the spiritual son of the third Karmapa, Rangjung Dorjé. At the time of the fourth Karmapa, the noble Rolpé Dorjé, he was the miraculous emperor of China, Tashing, who invited the sixteen elders, Virupa, and other masters [from India] to China.[9] At the time of the fifth Karmapa, the noble Déshin Shekpa, he was Situ Chökyi

Gyaltsen, the Karmapa's regent who was born within the family of [the holders of] Okmin Karma Monastery. During that lifetime, the Ming Dynasty emperor[10] gave him the [Chinese] title Kuanting Yen-tang Myau Tsi-gi Shir, meaning "The Loving Spiritual Master and World Leader Who Bestows Empowerment."[11] The emperor offered him this title, an imperial proclamation of his position, a crystal seal, and other gifts. From that time until the present, his title and position have remained undiminished. Both Tai Situ Tashi Namgyal, who lived during the time of the sixth Karmapa, the noble Tongwa Dönden, and Tai Situ Tashi Paljor, who lived during the time of the seventh Karmapa, Chödrak Gyatso, were born into the family of the Buddhist kings of Tibet and were venerated by the Chinese emperors. At the time of the eighth Karmapa, the noble Mikyö Dorjé, he was the well-known, highly learned and accomplished master Tai Situ Mitruk Chökyi Özer Gocha, proclaimed by the Karmapa, his teacher, to be a disciple identical to himself. At the time of the ninth Karmapa, Wongchuk Dorjé, he was Situ Chökyi Gyaltsen Gélek Pal-zangpo, proclaimed by Karmapa to be inseparable from him. Karmapa gave him a red crown radiant with gold, called the crown that liberates on sight.[12] He also entrusted the transmission of the inner meaning of the teachings to Tai Situpa, whose own lifework had a very significant spiritual influence. At the time of the tenth Karmapa, the noble Chöying Dorjé, he was his spiritual son, Chögyal Mipam Trinlé Rabten, who from a young age could uninhibitedly display higher perception and perform miracles, such as hanging his clothes on a ray of sunlight. At the time of the eleventh Karmapa, Yeshé Dorjé, he was Lekshé Mawé Nyima, who was nurtured spiritually by Karmapa and whose enlightened activity exhibited four means of liberation.[13]

At the time of the twelfth Karmapa, Jangchub Dorjé, he was Tai Situ Chökyi Jungné, who was empowered by the Karmapa as his regent of the true meaning of the transmission and who became the chief master of the thirteenth Karmapa. He showed

extreme kindness in this and other ways, extending the life of
the essence of the practice lineage teachings. Tai Situ Chökyi
Jungné was outstanding when compared to all other Tibetan
spiritual mentors of his time due to nine qualities: having been
foretold by holy persons; due to his innate abilities; his mastery of the study of scriptures; his reliance on erudite and accomplished mentors; his meditative cultivation, purification,
experience, and realization gained in the course of solitary re-
treats; his infallible understanding of the entire range of languages and subjects of Buddhist study; the influence of his
work; praise from all impartial spiritual mentors; and the numbers of disciples he nurtured.

At the time of the thirteenth Karmapa, the noble Dudul Dorjé,
he was Péma Nyinjé Wongpo, who was identical with the embodiment of all buddhas, Padmakara, Guru Rinpoché. He was
empowered by the Karmapa as his regent of the true meaning
of the transmission and became the chief master of the fourteenth Karmapa. His life of freedom demonstrated genuine
great accomplishment, and he exerted a great spiritual influence on the precious doctrine of the practice lineage. It might
have seemed that this noble master had completed his work
for the benefit of the world and was considering other aims
[i.e., had permanently passed away], but as it is said:

> The seven seas the dolphins roam
> May drain from time and waves,
> But Buddha's acts his heirs to serve
> No time will e'er erase.

Similarly, this master's compassionate presence in his disciples' lives has not diminished with time. He has simply
changed bodies: he has intentionally taken rebirth through his
infallible awareness as an illustrious protector of Buddhism and
guide for humanity. This master's brilliantly radiant physical
configuration of the marks and signs of enlightenment now
appears as the refuge and protector Tai Situ Péma Kunzang
Chökyi Gyalpo. *The Discourse Which Reveals Inconceivable Secrets* states:

Bodhisattvas who have attained the ultimate body of enlightenment do not experience birth, death, and rebirth. However, they manifest birth, death, and rebirth in order to bring beings to full spiritual maturity.

Further, *The Discourse Requested by Sagaramati* states:

The mind has been purified, with no stain remaining; therefore, it has the qualities of noncomposite phenomena, free of all stains. However, in order to bring others to full spiritual maturity, he or she intentionally retakes birth within the three realms.[14]

Further, the venerable Nagarjuna states:

Thus are the bodhisattvas:
Sure enlightenment they attained
But by compassion's force return
Until all awakening gain.

As is expressed in these quotations, our spiritual master has no attachment to his own benefit, the nectar of perfect peace. He has transcended ordinary existence but again takes rebirth within this world in a form of enlightenment made physically manifest. The circumstances of his reappearance — the details of the place of Tai Situpa's birth, his parents' family name, and the year — appeared vividly in the unhindered, pure vision of the wisdom of the great omniscient mighty victor [Karmapa, presumably the fourteenth] and were clearly predicted in his self-arisen adamantine speech:

Éma! [How wonderful!]
In the northern region of Tibet,
The Himalayan land,
The place the great god Tang-lha guards
Nam-Tang Plain, Lake Lhung-dri grand.
Around its banks stand families' tents,
Fine villages in deft design,
A place where many holy guides
Reached supreme attainment in their time:
Lotus-Born from Oddiyana,
Glorious Ga, the translator;
Gyalwé Lo Répa; and he

> Of the dark-red crown the bearer.
> In the northern quarter, near the east,
> A nomad's tent, the happy home,
> The parents by the name of Tsé;
> Of good families they are known.
> Their child born in wood-tiger year
> Took birth intentionally,
> To accomplish many goals
> For Buddhism and humanity.
> Marks and signs quite evident
> Will doubtful questions all appease:
> With faith, respect, and joy at heart
> Enjoy your mind's and body's ease.

The events surrounding the birth corresponded very closely to this prediction: he was born in just this region, to these parents, at the time mentioned; and the birth was accompanied by wonderful portents witnessed by all. Even during his childish play, he remembers places from his past lives and has unimpeded cognizance of the three times — the past, present, and future. These and other abilities provoke wonder in those fortunate to have a connection with him and confidence that the recognition of this reincarnation has been unmistaken.

Furthermore, the text of *The Group of Spiritual Instructions from Yel-puk at Namka Dzö* retrieved by the indisputably great treasure revealer of this time, Orgyen Chok-gyur Déchen Lingpa, states:

> In the year of the wood tiger,
> In Tang-lha's land, Lake Nam-tso near,
> My emanation, Samanta-bhadra,[15]
> Guide of beings, will appear.

This example, as well as others from texts retrieved at all the main treasure sources (such as Kandro Boom-dzong, Okmin Karma, Péma Shel-puk, and Seng-chen Namdrak) very clearly foretell this boy to be an incarnation of the master from Oddiyana, Guru Rinpoché. *The Great Prophecy of the Union of the Master's Enlightened Vision* states that following the six Tai Situpas who possessed the eyes of the spiritual instructions, six Tai Situpas who possess lotus tongues will spread the Buddha's doctrine. This incarnation is the second of the lotus-tongued Tai Situpas, and has been, from the very beginning of time, a regent of the king of spiritual instructions from Oddiyana, Guru Rinpoché. This protector of humanity has been enthroned on the lion throne of fearlessness by the sole father of all buddhas, the Lord of the World in human form, Karmapa. He has also been empowered as Karmapa's spiritual regent and entrusted with the essence of the true meaning of his teachings. This propitious and fortunate occasion is similar to the appearance of a buddha in the world: to see or to participate in such an event is extremely rare. Therefore it provides an appropriate occasion for all beings — gods and nagas, and humans in particular — to increase their cultivation of merit in a variety of ways, such as showing veneration by offering all their material possessions to this master. The manner that this can be done and the reason for doing so is explained in detail in all the discourses and tantras. For example, *The River of Salt Water Discourse* states:

> In the final age of five hundred years,
> In a master's form I will appear
> With "It is the Buddha!" in your mind,
> Respect me deeply at that time.

At this time of the end of the five-hundred-year periods of degeneration,[16] the Buddha will manifest as a spiritual mentor on many occasions. The powerful lord Virupa states:

> The master and Vajrasattva
> Separate can never be:
> The master's every master,
> Buddha, teaching, community.
> If it's for the state supreme
> Of accomplishment you yearn,
> Strive in every way you can
> The master's joyous mind to earn.
> The bearer of the vajra —
> All buddhas' forms in one —
> For our sake, in human form

At this time of conflict's come.
Know this and serve your master well
With all that's yours to give:
The buddhas of all times' great bliss —
The attainment you'll receive.

Thus he describes the master as the source of the union of
the Three Jewels. Offerings to the master constitute the highest
form of merit, as *The Vajra Heart Ornament Tantra* states:

Vajra Bearer, the master supreme,
Appears in our form through his skillful means.
Endeavor to please him: if you succeed,
You'll have made all the enlightened ones pleased.

A Section of the Root Tantra of the Wheel of Time states:

During ages past, present, future,
A million beings you've rescued
And offered gifts to jewels, three,
Yet in this life the goal eludes;
But if you please devotedly
Your master, sea of qualities,
Attainments common and supreme —
Yours in this life indeed!

The Five Stages of the Union of Secrets states:

Give up every offering
But those to your master made;
By pleasing him you will attain
The peak, all-knowing state.
By offering to the master,
Vajrasattva, highest guide,
What merit's left ungathered?
What yogic path unrealized?

How to act in relation to the master is explained in *Fifty Verses
in Praise of the Spiritual Master*:

Give always to the master
Who's like all enlightened ones,
With wishes to attain the state
Of awakening without end.
Give to the master humble gifts

Or any special, wondrous thing:
This will to every buddha be
A continuous offering;
Its accumulated merit
Will supreme attainment bring.

These and countless other passages from scripture emphasize that offerings given and veneration shown at all times to the illustrious spiritual master, the supreme Buddha Vajra Bearer (Vajradhara) incarnate, constitute the best and finest method of clearing away obscurations and of cultivating merit and wisdom. In particular, as mentioned above, this special occasion provides a unique and appropriate opportunity to actually practice the cultivation of merit.

This concludes a brief description of the main topic of this speech.

CHAPTER THREE

A Step-by-Step Description of Enthronement and the Presentation of Offerings

This section has three parts: (1) a general description of the acts which cultivate merit and wisdom, (2) the specific explanation of the content of the investiture of authority on the occasion of Tai Situpa's assumption of the great throne of spiritual instruction, and (3) in particular, the description of the main subject, the offering of the universe in the form of a mandala.

THE ACTS WHICH CULTIVATE MERIT AND WISDOM

The essential acts which the bodhisattvas must cultivate can be subsumed under two general categories: acts which cultivate merit and those which cultivate wisdom. *The Ornament of the Discourses* states:

> Bodhisattvas' cultivation:
> Merit, wisdom beyond compare.
> The first uplifts within existence,

The other ends emotions there.
Generosity and ethics
Are merit's accumulation
While wisdom's cultivated
By highest discrimination.
Forbearance, diligent exertion,
And meditation — the other three —
To both merit, wisdom's ranks
Belong together equally.
Steady practice constant virtue makes
By these five and wisdom's gathering:
This, Buddha's teachings' cultivation,
Will to success all wishes bring.

As stated, the practice of the six perfections, the essence of the cultivation of merit and wisdom, informs all acts which cultivate positive qualities and those which clear away negativity.

Moreover, in the present context, the sole aim of our spiritual practice on this occasion (principally the seven-part service) and all virtuous activity undertaken is to please our illustrious spiritual master, the embodiment of the essential union of all buddhas. Therefore, the cultivation of these two kinds of acts, which have the nature of the six perfections, occurs spontaneously. Further, each of even the most minor details that must be done with a pure motivation at this time is extremely beneficial and significant. For example, once the temple has been swept, decorations must be arranged and an excellent seat prepared on the throne of spiritual instruction. This is not done simply to create a magnificent setting; it is done for a special reason, as explained in the teachings included in the major [discourse] *The Sublime Pinnacle of Jewels*:

Where masters come to give the teachings true,
Prepare in the following manner:
Arrange his seat of the lion throne
Raise parasols and victory banners.
Array many kinds of offerings —
Pearls, cymbals' sounds, jewels, music sweet;
Pile cushions of many materials

On the Buddhist instruction seat.
Approach the abbots and masters
In this style enticing and elegant:
Have no regrets, for this service to others brings
The thirty-two marks of enlightenment.

Following this example, the effects of other acts are described in similar detail.

THE INVESTITURE OF AUTHORITY

The investiture of authority is performed through the assumption by our refuge and protector, the master who embodies the union of the essence of all buddhas, a supreme manifestation of enlightenment, Tai Situpa, of the great lion-supported throne upon which his predecessors turned the wheel of spiritual instruction. This investiture of authority and offering of consecration, held in connection with a service to cultivate positive qualities and a celebration, has three parts: (a) the preparation, (b) the main ceremony, and (c) the conclusion.

The Preparation

Just as the Honored One defeated malevolent influences before his attainment of the heart of awakening, all disruptive, misleading, interruptive disharmonious influences must be eliminated before the abundantly auspicious occasion of this investiture. In this case, this has already been done through the great powerful compassion of the chief of all circles of deities, the mighty sovereign, Karmapa.

Then Tai Situpa, the personification of the ten forces, the four forms of confidence, the four bases of miracles, the ten powers, and the four forms of enlightened activity[1] of the Joyful Ones, must be invited to the great throne of spiritual instruction, before which is spread a limitless array of offerings of the finest quality. This invitation is preceded by the visualized creation of a bathhouse and an actual ceremony of washing. This washing ceremony replicates two events. The first occurs when a universal monarch appears in the world: the elephant Airavata [the elephant ridden by Indra] descends from the thirty-third heaven carrying a jeweled container filled with nectar. The monarch is anointed and bathed with the nectar and thereby becomes invested with regal authority. The second occurs when the sovereign of spiritual instructions, the Honored One, the Buddha, is born in the world: the kings of the gods and nagas bathe his body with pure water from the heavens.

This washing ceremony clears away incidental illusory appearances of impurities and focuses in Tai Situpa all the special aspirations and enlightened activity of the Transcendent Ones and the bodhisattvas. Thus he will act as a supreme teacher to the gods and mankind until all cyclic existence comes to an end, without ever interrupting his activity of instruction, due to the illumination of his unlimited longevity and wisdom. All the radiance and blessing of the eternal circle of adornments of the enlightened body, speech, mind, qualities, and activities of the primordially existing buddhas and bodhisattvas who fill the expanse of space are focused and unalterably joined with the spiritual master by the seal of nondual union. This as well has already been done by the blessing of the omniscient Karmapa.

The Main Ceremony of Investiture
The main ceremony has two parts: (i) renewal of investiture of authority through ordinary offerings, and (ii) renewal of investiture of authority through special offerings.

Renewal of Investiture of Authority through Ordinary Offerings. This part of the main ceremony consists entirely of meritorious activity, beginning with a general cultivation of merit, a "seven-part service." In the first part, we imagine our bodies and those of all beings, whose numbers reach the limits of space, each multiplied to equal the number of molecules in all realms. All render homage to the master physically, verbally, and mentally with deep respect. Second, we offer actual and imagined offerings equal to the cloud-ocean of offerings presented to the buddhas by the bodhisattva Ever-Excellent (Samantabhadra). Third, we acknowledge with intense regret all our physical, verbal, and mental negative acts, obscurations, faults, and failings, and commit ourselves not to repeat them. Fourth, we rejoice in the fully positive acts done by spiritually advanced persons and by ordinary individuals. Fifth, we request that the wheel of true spiritual instruction, gathered in the three ways of spiritual development within Buddhism, be turned continuously. Sixth, we pray to the spiritual master to remain steadfast in his present physical form until the realms of cyclic existence come to an end. Seventh, we dedicate completely all the sources of past, future, or present virtue to the full awakening which does not fall into the two extremes.[2]

In particular during this stage of the investiture, a mandala offering of the entire universe is presented, followed in stages by such offerings as the representations of the eternal spontaneous circle of adornments of the body, speech, mind, qualities, and activities of enlightenment; special precious objects, such as expensive jewels and silk; and many different kinds of delicious food and drink. These are all intended as service and honor to the spiritual master.

Renewal of Investiture of Authority through Special Offerings. As is stated in *The Discourse Requested by Renowned as Pure*:

> Indra, among the offerings made to the Transcendent Ones, offerings of spiritual instructions are supreme. They are considered supreme, genuine, sublime, plentiful, best, and highest. Therefore, Indra, do not offer material things to me: offer spiritual instructions. Do not serve me with material objects: serve me with spiritual instructions and venerate me in this way.

Further, *The Flourishing of Great Liberation Discourse* states:

> Gifts of material objects represent generosity as practiced by the listeners. Such gifts create longevity and wealth but their effects will eventually be exhausted. Thus this generosity will not liberate one from cyclic existence. The gift of

the spiritual instructions of the Great Way creates in others the source of the aspiration to awaken and sustains the life of the wisdom of the three Buddhist ways of spiritual development.

Moreover, other discourses state:

A holy person's offering of spiritual instructions is the most sublime of all offerings.

One might fill the worlds in every direction within this three-thousand-realmed universe[3] to overflowing with priceless jewels and offer this. However, this gift is far exceeded by the offering of a suitable explanation of the meaning of only a four-line verse of genuine spiritual instruction. Although this describes the literal meaning of the offering of spiritual instructions, *The Discourse Requested by [Renowned as] Pure* from *The [Sublime] Pinnacle of Jewels* states:

The gift of spiritual instruction refers to the correct instruction of any scripture within the class of discourses, to upholding the scripture, to analyzing it, or to summarizing authentic spiritual instructions.

The offering that corresponds to this importance consists of six of the main Buddhist treatises. The first is *Entering the Middle Way* [by Chandrakirti], which presents the essence of all cycles of the Joyful One's spiritual realization. The book begins with a description of the philosophy of the perfection of wisdom — severance of the discursiveness inherent in relative reality — and emphasizes the profound nature of mind affirmed within the meditative state. Second, *The Highest Continuity* [by the bodhisattva Maitreya] begins with a definitive description of the nature of ultimate reality, the sphere of radiant wisdom, and emphasizes the expansive nature of mind as discerned in the postmeditative state. The third, *The Ornament of Realization* [by the bodhisattva Maitreya], begins with a description of the hidden meaning of the perfection of wisdom, the eight realizations,[4] and emphasizes the stages of the path of spiritual development practiced by the bodhisattvas. These three outstanding source texts explain the philosophy of the middle and final cycles of the Buddha's spiritual instruction.

Fourth, *The Treasury of Knowledge* [by Vasubandhu], the commentary on the collection of knowledge within the Buddha's teaching, presents a definitive description of the characteristics of all phenomena, principally a full explanation of the composites of experience — the psychophysical aggregates, the elements, and the sense faculties. Fifth is the root tantra of the Honored One, Joyful Vajra (Hevajra), *The Two Chapters*. This text is the sovereign of the yogini tantras, the highest pinnacle of the four classes of tantra of the secret mantra Vajra Way, itself superior from many perspectives to the common ways of spiritual development. Sixth, *The Profound Inner Meaning*, contains the great secrets from all classes of the highest yoga tantras, collected into one major work by the second Buddha, the venerable Rangjung Dorjé [the third Karmapa].

Lectures on the content of these excellent commentaries to the source texts, whose number equals the six perfections, create massive clouds of offerings of authentic spiritual instruction. Such lectures will be given by three upholders of the collections of the Buddha's teachings immediately following this reading. Diligent in their commitments, they have mastered the three trainings and are thus learned. Their teaching reflects the vast range of Buddhist scriptural sources. In debate, they can give rapid, convincing proofs. In their written works, the blessings of the [female bodhisattva of wisdom] Melodious One (Saraswati) resonate in their words: they illuminate the precious doctrine of the Buddha.

The Conclusion of the Investiture
The main part of the concluding ceremony involves a series of special offerings. The first is of the eight auspicious substances. To explain, immediately following the perfect enlightenment of our teacher [Shakyamuni Buddha] at Heart of Awakening

[Bodhgaya in north-central India], the bodhisattva Vajra-in-Hand (Vajrapani) presented him with a gift of white mustard seed. The other seven substances have been similarly consecrated as the source of all auspiciousness in the realms of existence and in the state of perfect peace. Moreover, when a universal monarch appears in the world, these substances are said to be offered to him to renew his authority. Further, the Vedas consider that meeting a person carrying yogurt (one of the eight) on a path is an extremely positive sign. These examples illustrate that these eight substances are the natural expression of virtue in material form. Therefore *The Sovereign Tantra of the General Empowerment of All Joyful Ones within the Vital Essence of Buddha Vairochana* contains a lengthy eloquent praise of these eight auspicious substances.

The second set of offerings, the eight auspicious symbols, were presented by the eight auspicious goddesses to the king of the gods, Indra, as a sign of his dominion after his complete triumph over the demigods. These eight are derived from the signs of perfection evident on the bodies of all buddhas. The third set of offerings, the seven precious articles of the monarch, include the sources of the power and the main wealth of universal monarchs who enjoy dominion over the entire world.[5]

To conclude the ceremony, prayers for auspiciousness are recited. These are sung joyfully in unison, principally by the omniscient mighty victor [Karmapa], who is surrounded by buddhas and bodhisattvas filling all space; by those filling the heavens, the gods and seers whose every word becomes true; by all awareness-holders and accomplished ones who have the power of higher perception and miracles; and by the assembled members of the virtuous community, to whom offerings are meritorious.[6] Their prayers, amidst a rain of flowers, produce virtuous and beneficial full illumination which pervades all places, times, and circumstances.

THE OFFERING OF THE UNIVERSE IN THE FORM OF A MANDALA

This section has eight parts, reflecting the excellent virtue of the auspicious number eight: (a) why the offerings of a mandala are considered the main form of offering, (b) the essence of the offering, (c) the literal meaning of the word *mandala*, (d) different styles of making the mandala offering, (e) the reasons for making this kind of offering, including the fact that the six perfections are complete within it, (f) directions for making the offering, (g) the visualization that accompanies it, and (h) what wishes should accompany the offering.

The Mandala: The Main Form of Offering

In general, the offering of the universe in the form of a mandala is considered the supreme of all offerings due to its purity and vastness from the perspectives of this offering's recipient, motivation, and substance. The recipient of the offering is not limited: the spiritual masters and the Three Jewels of every direction and time — past, future, or present — are imagined as the recipients. The motivation is not limited: since we make the offering striving for highest awakening, the common good of beings whose numbers fill all space is taken into consideration. The substance of the offering itself is not limited: any part of the universe within the limits of space and every offering therein are mentally gathered and made part of this vast offering. This offering avoids the impurities that contaminate material offerings during their preparation, the actual offering, or afterward, such as the impurity of thoughts of pride in having made a specific gift: this style of offering is particularly pure. As Lord Atisha states:

> Among all the ways of cultivating merit and wisdom through continual manual work, there is none more meritorious than the offering of mandalas.

Specifically, *An Approach to the Ultimate* states:

> Between the practice sessions three,
> Wash mouth, arms, legs quite thoroughly;
> Take flowers and then, before the master,
> Offer full mandalas of the Victors.

Fifty Verses in Praise of the Spiritual Master states:

> At three times with respect replete,
> Give mandalas with some flowers complete;
> With folded hands your teacher greet
> In honor, bow your head to touch his feet.

As stated here, we should make offerings of mandalas when meeting the spiritual master, when the wheel of spiritual instruction is turned, and when remembering our master. This activity pleases all enlightened ones and creates an auspicious connection to the eventual completion of the cultivation of merit and wisdom. The numerous outstanding vital features of this style of offering, such the importance of making it and the auspicious connections it creates, has made it the principal of all offerings in the Buddhist tradition.

The Essence of the Offering

When the mandala offering is made, the circular disc and the piles of offerings (of rice, etc.) act as symbols. According to the tradition of the discourses, they symbolize the full expanse of millions of configurations of the Supreme Mountain and the four continents of this world [described below], filled with clouds of various offerings from the pure lands of the buddhas in the ten directions. These are mentally gathered and offered to an infinite ocean of spiritual masters and the Three Jewels. According to the mantra tradition, the mandala symbolizes [four offerings]: the outer offering of all the appearances of this worldly realm; the inner offering which arises from the nature of the indestructible body; the "other" offering which includes these two as they appear spontaneously within the circles of configurations of meditation deities; and the ultimate offering of the nature of mind that dawns from the power of the supreme aspect present in all circumstances, the union of unchanging bliss and emptiness. If, through knowing this natural state of mind, we can understand the single essence of these offerings, all appearances which dawn as the symphony of the indestructible pure land of bliss and emptiness can be offered as the nature of outer, inner, other, and ultimate offerings.

The Literal Meaning of the Sanskrit Word Mandala

If the word *mandala* is explained literally, from the base, *mana* — "to know," the full-stop ending *da* (from components such as *an*) is added: the letters thus evolve into *manda*, meaning "what must be known," thus "essence," etc. When the beneficial component *la*, meaning "to hold" or "to have," is added, the word *mandala* is formed. This means, "the circle which holds the central essence."

Alternatively, to the base *madi* — "ornament," *num* (from the *iditra* components), *ach* (from the *kritra* components), and the beneficial component *la* can be added, giving *mandala*, meaning [in this case] "holding the pattern of the ornaments," which in this context refers to the pure realms.

The Styles in Which Mandalas Are Offered

Of the two types of mandalas — those used as a support for meditation[7] and those used for offering — this discussion concerns the latter, mandalas that are offered. Within the Original Tradition of secret mantra in the Himalayas, the seven-point mandala, consisting of the Supreme Mountain, the four continents, the sun, and moon, is the most widely known. Eleven-, fifteen-, and thirty-seven-point mandalas are all elaborations of this seven-point version. Within the source texts of profound instructions of Great Completion in particular, the mandala of the physical manifestation of enlightenment refers to the versions just mentioned; the mandala of enlightenment's form of perfect splendor consists of an eight-point configuration; and the mandala of ultimate enlightenment, a configuration of five points.

Within our New Tradition of Secret Mantra, many versions of mandalas are described in Indian source texts, including those by the master Sucharita and the mandala ritual by Nyokmé Pal. However, the principal version, based on the teachings of Kambala, the great master Buddhaguhya, and others, features twenty-three points: the Supreme Mountain, the four continents, their eight subcontinents, the seven precious articles of a universal monarch, a treasure vase, the sun, and the moon. Variations on this style have appeared — Jampal Drakpa substituted one's own body for the treasure vase, and Nyokmé Dorjé included an offering of sapphire and other jewels — but despite their unique features, these variations are essentially similar to the twenty-three-point version.

Many versions of the mandala offering spread here in Tibet, based on such teachings as Jétari's description of a seventeen-point mandala. Those practicing meditations on the Wheel of Time (Kalachakra) offer a nine-point mandala, adding the planets Rahu and Ketu to the seven-point version. Another possible variation is a twenty-five-point version, which is made by adding the same two planets to the twenty-three-point mandala. These two versions describe the Supreme Mountain, the continents, and other features of the world according to the Wheel of Time practice. All other versions, regardless of the number of points in the configuration, follow the description of the mountain and continents common to the discourses and the tantras, as described in the third chapter of *The Treasury of Knowledge*.

At present, the elaborate version of the mandala offering known throughout all schools and most widely used is one said to have been composed by the sovereign of spiritual life, Pakpa Rinpoché. In this version, offerings of the special wealth which distinguishes each continent, the eight goddesses (the goddess of charm, etc.), a parasol, and a victory banner are all added to the basic twenty-three-point version. This thirty-seven-point mandala offering has become the accepted practice [among Buddhists in the Himalayan region].

The Reasons for Offering a Mandala

This section provides an explanation, according to references from the scriptures, of how the six perfections are complete in every detail within the offering of a mandala and of the unique positive effects and importance of mandala offerings. *The Mandala Discourse* states:

> The mandala of Shakyamuni's made
> From six perfections' full array:
> Generosity — cow's urine, offerings;
> Ethics — the surface wiped and cleaned;
> Patience — insects found and set apart;
> Diligence — practice done with eager heart;
> Meditation — each moment of attention;
> Wisdom — the full blaze of its design.

Further in the same text:

> Your complexion will be golden;
> From all sickness you'll be freed;
> Far brighter than the gods or men,
> Your moon-like luminosity;
> Wealth and gold in full abundance;
> Born to Buddhist royalty;
> Yours the finest residence —
> All due to this activity.

The description of the benefits of the practice continues with:

> As it is said:
> Magnificent in wealth and body,
> Even friends reflect your splendor,
> Uplifted, by emotions untroubled,
> Your acts' course moves undeterred.

All these effects, which are similar to those of the six perfections, are produced by just one correct offering of a mandala.

Directions for Making the Offering

The ceremony of such a unique offering must be performed according to special guidelines to be followed impeccably. The best mandala disc is made of gold or silver; a moderately good one, from copper or iron; the least, from stone or wood. Since this is a special occasion, we must use a mandala disc made from the two most precious substances [gold and silver], ornamented by many unique designs.

The best substance to use for the piles of offerings on the disc is said to be jewels; the moderately good one, different kinds of grain; the least, sea shells. On this occasion, we offer jewels and pure grains dampened by saffron water, a symbol that the offerings are moistened by our aspiration to attain awakening. The surface of the disc is wiped clean of dust, an action that creates an auspicious connection to ensure that our offering will be without any fault whatsoever. To symbolize that all qualities will arise spontaneously from the foundation of the disc, water of cow excretions[8] mixed with saffron paste is sprinkled upon it. As the piles of offerings are placed on the disc, one's body, voice, and mind must remain sincere and respectful.

The Visualization That Accompanies the Offering

This section provides a brief description of the series of the special and most important visualizations that accompany the offering of this mandala of the universe. To begin, the hundred-syllable mantra of Vajrasattva is recited while the surface of the disc is wiped three times in a clockwise direction. During this, we imagine that negative acts, obscurations, sicknesses, disruptive influences, and interruptions to spiritual development that have been accumulated within our own and others' experience since beginningless time are cleansed and purified.

While repeating the [Sanskrit] formula *om vajra bhumi ah hum*, we imagine the supporting discs of the elements[9] covered by this world-system's foundation, called Great Power. This foundation is made of gold, pleasing to the touch, and extremely vast. During the single repetition of *om vajra réké ah hum*, we imagine the circular range of iron mountains which marks the boundary of the foundation.

The offering ritual described here is a concise version: such details as the creation of each feature of the visualization from seed syllables are unnecessary. Instead, we imagine each feature, such as the central mountain and the continents, at the moment its corresponding pile of rice is placed on the offering disc.

At the center of the disc stands the square, massive Supreme Mountain, which has four terraces. Each side of the mountain is made of a dazzling jewel which lends its color to the sky in that quarter: the eastern side is made of crystal; the southern, of beryl; the western, of ruby; and the northern, of gold. Seven consecutive square ranges of golden mountains surround the massive central mountain like a series of curtains. Their names are (from the innermost): Yoke, Plough, Acacia Forest, Pleasing-to-See, Horse Ear, Bending, and Horizon. Swirling oceans of water with eight qualities fill the area between the ranges. These eight qualities are listed in *The Transmission of Discipline*:

> Cool and tasty, light and soft,
> Clear, pure, the stomach's pleasure,
> When one drinks, the throat's unharmed:
> Eight qualities this water's measure.

At the summit of the massive mountain, a tower is located in each of the four cardinal directions; at its center stands the city Beautiful-to-Behold, where the Victorious Residence is situated. Parks, such as the Park of Various Chariots, extend along each of the four sides of the city. In the northeast stands the wish-fulfilling tree, Ground-Sprung Completeness, in front of which lies a stone slab called Amolika. The Gathering Place Where the Gods Hear the Excellent Doctrine is located in the southwest. These details provide some examples of the unique features of the wealth and splendor in the gods' world. These must be recalled immediately after the Supreme Mountain is offered.

Then, in unison with the words of offering, piles of rice are placed on the offering disc to represent the four continents: the

semicircular eastern continent of Majestic Body, the trapezoi-
dal southern continent of Land of Jambu, the round western
continent of Bountiful Cattle, and the square northern continent
of Unpleasant Sound. Each continent has the color of the side
of the Supreme Mountain it faces. Smaller continents are situated on either side of each of the four continents: Body and
Majestic Body in the East, Tail-Fan and Other Tail-Fan in the
South, Movement and Treading the Perfect Path in the West,
and Unpleasant Sound and Moon of Unpleasant Sound in the
North. These eight sub-continents share the color and shape of
their neighboring continents but are smaller in area.

The eastern continent is filled with mountains of jewels and
other precious substances, such as beryl and gold. A thick forest of wish-fulfilling trees which provide all needs and desires
grows on the southern continent. On the western continent a
pair of cattle, a cow and a bull, provide an inexhaustible sup-
ply of whatever the residents of the continent wish. The northern continent is filled to overflowing with a harvest that needs
no cultivation. The foods there have one hundred flavors and a
thousand nutritious elements, and relieve sickness and disor-
ders as well as hunger and thirst.

Spiritual masters have used the following citation from *The
Illustrious Gathering* as a reference for their practice of including the seven precious articles among the offerings of the
mandala:

> The learned fill this earthly realm
> With monarch's riches to the skies
> To receive attainment in return,
> They're offered daily by the wise.

When a universal monarch appears in the world, the force
of his merit creates these seven precious articles as part of the
wealth of his royal domain. The following description of the
seven is based upon passages found in *The Great Enjoyment
Discourse*, *The Treasury of Knowledge*, and *The Transmission of
Discipline*.

The precious wheel is made of gold and other essences of divine substances. Its circumference and center are perfectly round; it holds one thousand fine spokes in its circle. No artisan fashioned it: it appeared by itself. This wheel can rise into the air and travel a distance of 1,000,000 *yojanas* a day.[10] It can control all the continents and has many other unique qualities.

The precious jewel is of beryl and has three distinctive qualities: it has eight facets, and equals the measure of a large man's thigh; it is dazzlingly bright; and its radiance reaches ten miles in every direction, lighting both the day and night. Moreover, when one is thirsty, water of the eight qualities flows from the jewel. Within the radius of one thousand *yojanas* around it, sicknesses and untimely death do not occur.

The precious queen was born to the aristocracy; her body and complexion are beautifully attractive. Her breath has the scent of lotus flowers; her pores exude the fragrance of sandalwood. Like the finest silk, her skin is delightful to touch, warm in cold weather, cool in the heat. She follows the path of virtue and does nothing reprehensible. She has renounced the thirty-two faults of women and is wealthy in positive qualities.[11]

The precious government minister has four distinctive qualities. His faculties are clear and attentive. With the eyes of a god, he is able to spot treasure within an area of ten miles and retrieves many jewels with ease: thus the royal treasury is never exhausted. He listens to the orders of the king and obeys his commands. He is able to anticipate the king's wishes so that he fulfills them even without having been delegated to a task. In all his acts he causes no harm to others.

The precious elephant has eight distinctive qualities. His four hooves, tail, genitals, and trunk all rest evenly on the ground. His body is large, well formed, delightful to look at, and stable. He is white in color, like the glow of a water lily, and is able to fly through the sky. He is thrilled at the sight of the king, whose wishes he knows and whose orders he obeys. His limbs are all very firm. He is able to enter battle on land, sea, or air and can defeat all enemies. In one day he can circle the Land of Jambu. He goes wherever the king wishes, without having to be commanded. The crown of his head carries a golden victory banner, and his body is covered with a golden net.

The precious horse has eight distinctive qualities. His color is that of a peacock's neck, both attractive and amazing to see. His form is magnificent. He is able to circle the king's territory and to return in just one morning or to circle the Land of Jambu three times a day. He has no sickness, temporary or chronic; his body has many perfect marks, such as a jewel at his forehead. He is able to fly through the sky. He shows respect toward the king when mounted. He possesses many miraculous powers.

The precious general has eight distinctive qualities. His faculties are clear and attentive. He fulfills the king's wishes without having been asked. He has full expertise in the martial arts. He has renounced any act done for his own benefit and is not attached to any particular policy for the benefit of others: he remains faithful to his rank. When in battle against enemies, he knows the right time to attack or to retreat. Thus he enjoys the power and glory of victory in battle.

Another offering included in the mandala is the excellent vase, an inexhaustible wish-fulfilling source of precious substances such as diamonds, sapphires, emeralds, gold, and silver.

The supreme offering of the eight goddesses who impart pure bliss to all buddhas is made according to the system of yoga tantra. The goddess of charm is white and holds her fists at her sides. The goddess of garlands is yellow and carries garlands of flowers and precious jewelry. The goddess of song is pink, plays a guitar, and sings songs such as those with seven intonations. The goddess of dance is multicolored and performs many different dances. The goddess of flowers is white and carries bouquets of white lotuses and other flowers. The goddess of incense is yellow and holds an incense container overflowing with such sweet smells as those of aloe-wood and sandalwood. The goddess of lamps is light red and carries a jeweled lamp which shines like the sun and moon. The goddess of perfume is green and sprinkles perfumed water from a conch shell filled with pure water mixed with camphor, saffron, and other scents. All eight goddesses are beguilingly attractive: their bodies are supple, their movements fluid, and their smiles dazzling. They wear all manner of ornaments fashioned from silk and jewels.

Other offerings are those of the circles of the sun and moon, located in the sky by the eastern and western continents, respectively. The sun's basic composition is of precious fire-crystal, encircled by a ring of gold. Its circumference measures fifty-one *yojanas*. The moon's basic composition is of precious water-crystal, encircled by a ring of silver. Its circumference measures fifty *yojanas*. Both have the unique qualities of the wealth of the gods.

Above the southern and northern continents, respectively, stand the precious parasol and the victory banner. The parasol is crowned by a jewel, is made of a variety of precious substances, and has a handle of gold. The banner of heroic victory over every foe has a special top, a jeweled handle, and flowing silks.

Other offerings made at this time include the eight substances (*durva* grass, a mirror, etc.) which mark auspicious events, the eight auspicious signs (the vase, the knot, etc.), the seven semi-precious articles (the sword, the snake skin, etc.),[12] objects that please the five senses, the extracted essence of immortality, medicine that heals sickness, the forms of service given to an important person, a throne, cushions, clothes, jewelry, and various necessary articles. We fill the world to overflowing with the entire range of the pleasures to be found among the riches of gods and human beings. Similarly we imagine that we fill the vast expanse of worlds in the ten directions with the same special offerings. Our offerings equal those of the Buddha and the bodhisattvas who have reached the highest stages of awakening: the power of their perfect liberation, aspirations, and intention create the design and the substance of an expansive cloud of offerings equal to the drops in an ocean, unlimited in both extent and measure. These should be offered with the far-reaching and sincere intention that the offerings continue uninterruptedly until the ends of space and time.

The Wishes That Should Accompany the Offering

How should we direct our wishes when we make such an important offering? In general, we should do as the master Ashvaghosha states:

> Think not of virtue done with hopes for fame,
> For acclaim, or joys of gods and men;
> Reject all thought of worldly profit —
> Dedicate good to transcendent ends!

As stated, if meritorious acts lack the directed intention of transcendent skillful means — great compassion — and discernment — appreciation of emptiness — they simply become part of the worldly cycle of cause and result. Of these two, appreciative discernment of profound emptiness stands alone as the crucial determining factor. On the subject of profound discriminating awareness, it is said:

> For as long as your virtue has not been perfected,
> Realizing true emptiness can't be expected!

Although emptiness cannot be directly realized until a great accumulation of virtuous activity has been completely perfected, it is possible to understand a philosophy that accords with this realization. The bodhisattva Shantideva states:

> When the concrete and the abstract
> And thinking cease to entertain,
> With neither object nor objective,
> The mind in perfect peace remains.

This means we should not entertain any common discursive thought in our minds, nor should we reflect upon abstract emptiness. We thereby transcend both material form, which exhibits characteristics, and the realm of the abstract without characteristics. By resting without fixation in the essence, emptiness, our cultivation of merit becomes pure. As an example of this, *Entering the Path to Awakening* states:

When attachment is relinquished
To the gift, the giving, and giftee,
"A transcendent perfection,"
The name that's given to this deed.

In this case, the original natures of the [spiritual master,] recipient of the offering of the mandala; of what is offered [the mandala itself]; and of ourselves, the offerers, are undifferentiated by distinct characteristics: this common nature is the sphere of perfect simplicity. While we remain in meditative equanimity within this essence of our own awareness, free from concepts of recipient, offering, and doer, the offerings continue to be made through the uninhibited appearance of the interconnectedness of events which unfold as an illusion. This style of giving (and similar performance of the other perfections), guided by the eyes of discriminating awareness as described, constitute the simultaneous cultivation of merit and wisdom, the highest form of virtue.

Specifically, we should direct our wishes in the following specific manner:

As it is said,
Since all things' arising depends on conditions,
Phenomena rest on the highest intentions![13]

and

...the spiritual influence of the undivided intention of the
Buddhist community....

These quotations indicate that rather than being rendered diffuse by individual interests, the harmonious intention that directs this virtuous activity should be held in common by all participants. To begin with, the recipient of this special, vast offering must not be made subject to partiality. We should be decisive in our appreciation of our illustrious spiritual master, the great Buddha Vajra Bearer, Tai Situpa, as the complete expression in a single form of the entire extent of the ocean of precious buddhas, whose numbers fill all space. The heart of the activity described in this text is the presentation of offerings to this master with deep respect and with prayers for the following desired results: that the precious teaching of the Buddha, both in scripture and in realization, should spread, flourish, and long remain in every manner and in every region; that every noble, impartial person who sustains these teachings should remain in this world and in harmony with other Buddhist leaders; that the gatherings of the Buddhist community in every region should grow and their enlightening activity of the three trainings and the two cycles[14] should steadily increase without diminishing, like lakes swelling during the springtime; that even the names of any sign of degeneration of the world's condition, such as epidemics, famine, weapons, or battles, should be unheard of in this region and country, and throughout the whole world; and that every form of the four kinds of magnificent wealth[15] — longevity, prosperity, power, etc. — should increase as they do during a perfect age. We also gather and focus all the virtuous activity we have done at this time with that of all the virtuous activity we have ever done. We pray that by its power and spiritual influence, the bodies, voices, and minds of our places of refuge, the illustrious, highest protectors and guides of the beings of the three worlds, the glorious mighty victor, the great Karmapa, and the all-knowing and all-seeing loving protector Tai Situpa, together with their lineage of spiritual heirs, may remain in this world like indestructible vajras, like eternal seals, and like unalterable victory banners! May they be free from the changes of birth or death, defeat or destruction, until the sun of the Buddha Loving-Kindness dawns in this world! May they continue to enjoy constant and stable well-being forever! May they beat the great drum of profound and vast spiritual instructions! May they sound the conch shell of the Buddha's teaching! May they cause a rain of teachings to descend! May they truly raise the victory banner of Buddhism! By their doing so, may the long and faultless tradition of the practice lineage, the Karma Kamtsang,[16] in its cycles of study, meditation practice, and activity, spread, fully increase, and remain in every part of this great world where Jambu [rose apple] trees grow, until the wheel of spiritual instructions of the fifth guide of the Fortunate Eon, the Buddha Loving-Kindness, fills the world. This concludes the intention upon which I request this gathering of the Buddhist community, the field for the cultivation of merit and wisdom, to give their undivided attention during the stages of the mandala offering of the universe to our spiritual master.

Dedication and Colophon

Writing begs the erudition
Found in sayings of the wise;
Fools who cunningly spout prattle
Seek joy in vain from holy eyes.

One's own side acclaimed with slyness,
Others' views decried with scorn —
Delicious food with poison mixed —
To readers' hearts a deadly thorn.

But if genuine narrations
Which impartial judges deem correct;
You still find unacceptable,
Blame your crooked intellect!

Those who congregate and celebrate
Where no words sublime are said —
A silent herd at waters' edge —
From noble traditions have strayed.

The practice lineage sun has dawned;
Its followers good fortune now enjoy —

This knowledge now must be proclaimed,
Work my rare spare time employs.

May the minds of those who speak the teachings
Blossom from this simple lecture's seeds;
May the world with perfect words be filled —
Honey in the throats of clever bees!

*This text was written by Karma Ngawang Yonten Gyatso (Jamgon
Kongtrul) on the occasion of the investiture of the supreme reincarnation of the loving protector, the great Buddha Vajra Bearer, Tai
Situpa, on the lion throne of spiritual instruction at his main monastic seat, Palpung Monastery. This book represents a tiny fraction of
what could be expressed by those who appreciate the significance of
this event.*

May virtue increase! May all be auspicious!

Appendix: On Spiritual Kings and Crowns

This appendix contains two documents which supplement the main text. The first is a translation of the transcript of an undated speech by Jamgon Kongtrul, given to introduce the presentation of the red crown by one of the Tai Situpas, likely the young Péma Kunzang, whose enthronement ceremony was preceded by the reading of the main text above. The red crown and the ceremony of its presentation remain one of the trademarks of the Tai Situpas. As is clear in the following text, the Tai Situpas draw their inspiration and example for their crown from the leader of the lineage, the Karmapa, whose black crown similarly serves as one of that master's unique and characteristic possessions.

The second text translated below provides a brief account of the short life of Tai Situpa Péma Kunzang. This biography is a small extract from *The History of the Kagyu Lineage*, a book published recently in eastern Tibet (Kham), the work of a group of modern Tibetan scholars. Tai Situpa's life story is followed by a short note from Jamgon Kongtrul's *Autobiography* which describes his part in the funeral arrangements for the young master

The Twelfth Tai Situpa, Péma Donyö Nyinjé, presents the Red Crown.
(Photo: Sherab Ling Buddhist Institute)

who had been so important to him. A list of the birth and death years of the series of Karmapas' and Tai Situpas' incarnations follows.

THE RED CROWN OF THE TAI SITUPAS

A Brief Introduction on the Occasion of the Presentation of the Precious Red Crown Which Liberates on Sight, Describing the Reasons for and the Benefits of Seeing It

Today I address myself to all present, be you of high, low, or middle stations in life: in general, to those of you who are imbued with faith and devotion, whose virtue is reflected in your intentions and your deeds, and specifically, to the principal members of this gathering, the wealthy patrons who have sponsored this event.

As [the Buddha] said in *The Declarations*,

> There, in worlds where live the wise,
> Faith and wisdom's honored place —
> Their wealth sublime in wise men's eyes,
> Common gems they view as base.

The most sublime of all work and wealth are the faith found in the study of the qualities of enlightenment and the wisdom born of the comprehension of their causes. To increase these, I would like to offer you a little information pertinent [to today's event].

In general, all buddhas possess both skillful means and great compassion; therefore from within the sphere of totality, complete simplicity, they take the forms of the body of enlightenment's perfect splendor. Each symbol and aspect of their bodies, pure lands, ornaments, and possessions — such as their thrones and ways of gazing — guide an inconceivable number of beings toward enlightenment. Further, they appear in impure realms as the play of forms of manifest enlightenment, be these created, or ordinary beings, or supreme manifestations. These appear in relation to the bodies, voices, and minds of ordinary beings: the buddhas' bodies, their voices' speech, their

minds' reflections, and their talents and activities' ways of appearing share no common pattern, yet in their varied forms
they lead the variety of beings to uplifting spiritual paths and
to those which lead to certain satisfaction.[1]

Since the bounds of space and the constituent natures of sentient beings exceed measure and limits, for the sake of all beings, all enlightened ones manifest in numbers equal to the par-
ticles within a buddha's pure land, on each particle within the
pure land. However, their methods of guiding those they set
out to spiritually nurture do not conform to a single set pattern. In some realms, they appear as buddhas, bodhisattvas,
listeners, and solitary sages; in others, only one of such forms
appears and gives spiritual instructions through spoken words
or symbols. In some realms, they guide as seers, Brahmins,
Brahma, Indra, or universal monarchs. In some realms, they
give spiritual guidance to sentient beings as radiant light; in
some, as blossoming or closing lotus flowers; and in others, as
the scent of incense. Such an infinite variety of ways have been
described in the precious discourses [of the Buddha].

If the single example of the enlightened activity of the
bodhisattva Mighty All-Seeing One (Avalokiteshvara) is taken
to illustrate this, on each pore of his body appear an infinite
number of pure lands of the Buddha, of varying size, shape,
and design, each manifesting a corresponding spiritual guide.
Further, it can be learned from authoritative sources that this
bodhisattva has created limitless emanations to spiritually guide
others in ways appropriate to each. All of these manifestations
teach spiritual instructions in their own languages, such as the
king of horses, Balaha, on the island of the cannibal demonesses;
and the king of flies in the city of swamp-demons. Moreover,
in the land of the spiritually exalted [India], his emanations as
lords of meditative accomplishment during their conduct of
tantric discipline employed different styles of miracles, songs
of vajra realization, and transmission of their mind's wisdom
to lead an infinite number of beings to complete liberation. In
Tibet, he appeared as manifest bodies of enlightenment in

ordinary human form, such as the three ancestral Buddhist kings,[2] their wives, children, and government ministers; as artistically created manifest bodies of enlightenment, of which the principal one is the wish-fulfilling gem, Jowo Shakyamuni;[3] and as the past and present erudite and accomplished spiritual guides of every school whose lives of freedom, although not conforming to a specific pattern, have been entirely of tremendous service to Buddhism and to beings.

Specifically, on the subject of the origin of helping others through the presentation of crowns, the second buddha, the great master from Oddiyana, Guru Rinpoché, praised in adamantine speech the measureless benefits, for both the wearer and the viewer, of crowns belonging to the three, five, or other numbers of buddha-families. Further, he who was prophesied by the Victor, the incomparable doctor from Dawkpo, Gampopa, described in detail the similar qualities of the three crowns to benefit the doctrine and those of the meditation crown in particular. Therefore, these crowns have become commonly used in all branches of the Kagyu and Nyingma traditions. Any of those crowns, however, is surpassed by the particularly outstanding meaning and usefulness of the precious black crown which liberates on sight, one of the principal forms of the enlightened activity of the Lord of the World, the illustrious Karmapa, who through his series of lives places many beings on the stage of no-return to cyclic existence through sight, hearing, remembering, or touch.

This crown's origins date to the moment an emanation of All-Seeing One, a seer named Rare Birth, attained vajralike meditative absorption: as a sign of empowerment, the victors and their spiritual heirs placed on his head a vajra crown made of the hair from the heads of ten million wisdom dakinis. Since that time, the crown has remained [invisibly but] inseparably on the head of each member of the series of his reincarnations — such masters as the bodhisattva Matiratna, the great accomplished one Saraha, and the illustrious Dusum Kyenpa — but apart from the few who had the karma and a fortunate connection to the master, it was difficult to see the crown. Therefore, a manifestation of the bodhisattva Gentle Melody (Manjushri), the Ming emperor of China, Yung-lo, prayed to the fifth Karmapa, the mighty victor Déshin Shekpa, and offered him the black crown which liberates on sight, known as "the light of the world," made according to the emperor's sight of the crown.[4] Karmapa consecrated it to be inseparable with his naturally appearing crown of wisdom: thus the crown appeared within the experiential domain of all persons, high and low.

Later, as the fifth Garwong[5] stated:

> Master and disciples, in perfecting genuine inter-
> relation,
> Have joined their mind-streams in the meaning's
> realization.
> The inseparable master and disciples, Karmapa...

In the pure lands, the master, Karmapa, and his disciples appear as the Buddha Infinite Light (Amitabha), the bodhisattvas All-Seeing One, the protector Loving-Kindness, Lord of Secrets (Vajrapani) and others, the minds of this teacher and his entourage inseparable. In either India or Tibet, wherever the body of the great mighty victor Karmapa has been born, the others have joined their minds with his as one by reincarnating with him and perfecting the three ways of pleasing their master.[6] The mighty victor, the omniscient Karmapa, placed red crowns with a golden glow which liberate on sight on the heads of the previous incarnations of the victor Gargyi Wongpo, the protector Loving-Kindness Tai Situpa, and Lord of Secrets Gyaltsab. These crowns indicate their empowerment as masters inseparable with the three mysteries [thought, word, and deed] and the enlightened activity of Karmapa's series of incarnations. He then authorized them as chieftains of his enlightened activity which is renowned throughout the world. Thus, the red and black crowns have the same shape, a symbol that no difference exists between the mind and qualities of the father [Karmapa] and those of his spiritual sons. The slight differences in the colors and designs of the crowns show that each maintains his individual skillful enlightened activity. Therefore, whether one sees the red or black crown makes no difference whatsoever in the benefit of doing so, the four means of liberation.[7]

In particular, when the omniscient Tai Situpa resides in the heaven of Joyful as the Buddha's regent Protector Loving-Kindness, he wears a crown decorated with jewels. Simply the sight or thought of this crown clears away the two obscurations, and causes the meditative absorption of illuminating great love to develop in the viewer's mind. Further, when he reveals himself as Guru Padmakara [Guru Rinpoché] in the great celestial palace, Lotus Light, he always wears a crown, such as the lotus crown called the Crown Which Overpowers Common Appearances, which symbolizes the chief of his buddha family, Buddha Infinite Light. This and other crowns effortlessly rain on their viewers the four empowerments' blessing of adamantine wisdom. When Tai Situpa acts as the master of the precious doctrine of the practice lineage in the Himalayan region, the crowns [worn by Loving-Kindness and Guru Rinpoché] mentioned above are transformed into the red crown with a golden glow which Tai Situpa has used widely to perform the enlightened activity of the four liberations.

When a universal monarch gains possession of the thousand-spoked wheel of gold, dominion over the four continents is his. In the same fashion, when one sees these precious crowns which bring liberation on sight worn by the victor, Karmapa, or his spiritual heirs as mentioned above, special benefits are accrued, the results of their special enlightened intention and activity. It is just as the great accomplished master Karma Pakshi [the second Karmapa] stated:

> When crowns are by their bearers worn,
> Who sees, in low realms won't be born.

It is possible to consider that bestowal of empowerments, spiritual instruction, and the like represent partial ways of helping beings. In those cases, if an individual has all his or her senses intact, develops comprehension, does not break the tantric commitments, and maintains faith and devotion, he or she will be led from happiness to happiness. On the other hand, those same events can also provide the opportunity for those who have no faith and those who have broken commitments or maintain mistaken views to create the causes for future rebirth in the miserable existences. Thus, empowerments or instructions and so forth can create both positive and negative effects. However, the benefits of viewing this precious crown which liberates on sight does not depend on whether all one's senses are intact, on whether one has kept one's commitments or not, nor on gender, nor on age, nor on any other distinction: to the extent one's eyes see the crown, the seeds of freedom will be planted; to the extent one hears [of it], virtuous tendencies will be formed; and to the extent one thinks of it with faith, blessings will effortlessly develop. If one offers wealth such as material offerings, if one expresses devotion in prostrations, circumambulations, and prayers; or even if one just throws a flower in the crown's direction, one will complete a great cultivation of merit. What is more, even those with mistaken views will later find the path to freedom. As Shantideva stated:

> Those who to their tormentors
> Bring connections to bliss —
> I seek refuge in such as they,
> The source of every happiness.

This being the case, everyone here should view the crown with single-minded faith, devotion, and respect. Prayers done at this time with this attitude will have the same effect as prayers made to a wish-fulfilling jewel for any temporal or ultimate accomplishments one desires: they will surely be effortlessly and spontaneously answered during this life, during the next life, or in between, according to the capability and connection of each person. I ask that everyone of any station in life keep this in mind so that you do not waste this human life you have attained and this opportunity to see the precious crown which liberates on sight. I offer these words to you today in the hope that each of you will dedicate yourself to virtuous activity, each according to his or her ability, strength, and means, so that you further increase in your stream of being a great cultivation of merit and wisdom.

Composed by Guna [Sanskrit for the Tibetan word Yonten, part of one of Kongtrul's names, Yonten Gyatso].

Sarva Mangalam! [May all be auspicious!]

THE TENTH TAI SITUPA, PÉMA KUNZANG

> In the year of the wood tiger,
> In Tang-lha's land, Lake Nam-tso near,
> My emanation Samantabhadra,
> Guide of beings, will appear.

As predicted in the vajra scriptures of the treasure texts, this indisputable accomplished master was born in the wood tiger year of the fourteenth cycle, by the banks of Lake Nam-tso, in front of the northern Tang-lha plain. Once the reincarnation was identified by the fourteenth Karmapa, Kongtrul Yonten Gyatso traveled to central Tibet, where he requested custody of the child from the government and from Sera Monastery,[8] and then invited him to Palpung Monastery.

For his education, Situ Péma Kunzang relied upon such masters as the great scholar of Buddhist traditions Tashi Özer. From an early age he displayed spontaneous mastery of miracles and higher perception. Through the activity of his accomplishment, he crossed the Dri [Yangtse] River in high season on horseback, descended the Heaven's Ladder at the retreat center on horseback, and rode an untamed horse from Dergé to Palpung Monastery in two hours.[9] Many persons found flowers in the horse's hoofprints; it is said that Kyentsé Rinpoché had some of these in his possession.

In Den-kok, one person leading a wild bull met Tai Situpa on a road. He remarked, "Don't keep that bull of yours!" The man ignored him, thinking, "What won't such a wild monk say?" Later that bull killed the man.

Once, when traveling to Tibet province, a river was swollen to the mountainsides by monsoon rains. Everyone said it would be impossible to cross the river and began to pitch their tents. Tai Situpa gave everyone a fierce scolding: all the persons in the camp entered the torrent and reached the far side without incurring any harm whatsoever.

Although such stories about Péma Kunzang were common, everyone criticized him as being "the wild Situ." In response, the noble spiritual master Jamyang Kyentsé Wongpo lauded him, saying, "He is really the precious master from Oddiyana [Guru Rinpoché] in the flesh." I have heard that an account of his life of freedom was written, but I have not seen it. Although he was generally given to wild behavior, such as wearing masks and costumes, drinking alcohol, competing in horse races, and shooting rifles, because all the Tai Situpa's incarnations have appeared only as holders of pure monastic discipline, this propensity led him to scrupulously avoid sexual relationships.

Finally, at the age of thirty-two, in the wood bird year (1885), he went to visit the noble master Jamyang Kyentsé Wongpo at Dzong-sar. On the return journey, he commanded the butcher of Chötri Shi, Boom-chung Tak-gyal, "Lead my horse and walk." At the gate of [his?] residence, Péma Kunzang got off his horse, called Trang-nak, an incomparable horse of the finest breed, and gave it to the butcher, saying, "From now on, renounce all killing!" The man did as he was ordered, thus ensuring that for him the doors to rebirth in miserable realms were closed.

This kind of seemingly disordered behavior was not due to mental confusion: Péma Kunzang had intentionally taken rebirth in this world. However it is possible that each of the leaders of the Kagyu doctrine is obstructed by evil spirits[10] during their tenth incarnations: thus, great holy individuals have explained that his acts were ways of reversing those negative influences.

At the age of thirty-two, during the wood bird year of the fifteenth cycle (1885), the display of his manifestation momentarily dissolved. (*History of the Kagyu Lineage*, 240-243)

In his *Autobiography*, Jamgon Kongtrul adds this sad and sour note to end the story of this young master:

> On the sixth day of the twelfth month [of 1885], the venerable supreme manifestation of enlightenment [i.e., Tai Situpa, Péma Kunzang] departed from Palpung Monastery to the realm of peace. Since I had experience in how to prepare memorial ceremonies and other [aspects of funerals], Ön-gen Tulku sent a messenger with a letter requesting that I come immediately to the monastery. This I did. Ceremonies of offering to the spiritual master before his physical remains were done for only three days.[11]
>
> Although we have a master copy of a book containing the details of the funeral ceremonies for the last two Situ Rinpochés, the temper of the time finds us without any of the major possessions of [the Tai Situpas listed in the book], either in the main residence, the administration, or close to the body of the spiritual master. To ensure that whatever is left will not be dispersed, I made a list of all of the articles offered during the memorial services. An account of the cremation and a detailed list of Tai Situ's estate — the sacred supports, clothes, possessions, etc., at both his upper and lower residences — was written in a register by Ön-gen Rinpoché together with the monastic administrators. Money to begin construction of a memorial stupa was deducted [from this], and the noble from Ga, Dro-dok, was pressed into taking responsibility for it. (*page 168a.2-6*)

Kongtrul lived to meet and to enthrone the eleventh Tai Situpa, Péma Wongchuk Gyalpo, who lived a relatively long life — 66 years — and entered into the main lineage of the Karmapa's Oral Instruction Lineage as the principal spiritual master to the highest lamas of his time, including the sixteenth Karmapa and Kalu Rinpoché.

THE INCARNATIONS OF KARMAPA AND TAI SITUPA

Karmapa	Tai Situpa
1. Dusum Kyenpa (1110-1193)	Drogon Réchen (1148-1218)
2. Karma Pakshi (1206-1283)	Yeshé Ö (13th century)
3. Rangjung Dorjé (1284-1339)	Ratna Bhadra (14th century)
4. Rolpé Dorjé (1340-1383)	Tashing, Chinese emperor (?Toghon Temur, 1320-1370)
5. Déshin Shek-pa (1384-1415)	1. Chökyi Gyaltsen (1377-1448)
6. Tongwa Donden (1416-1453)	2. Tashi Namgyal (1450-1497)
7. Chödrak Gyatso (1454-1506)	3. Tashi Paljor (1499-1541)
8. Mikyö Dorjé (1507-1554)	4. Chökyi Gocha (1542-1585)
9. Wongchuk Dorjé (1555-1603)	5. Chökyi Gyaltsen (1586-1657)
10. Chöying Dorjé (1604-1674)	6. Chögyal Mipam Trinlé Rabten (1658-1682)
11. Yeshé Dorjé (1676-1702)	7. Lekshé Mawé Nyima (1683-1698)
12. Jangchub Dorjé (1703-1732)	8. Chökyi Jungné (1700-1774)
13. Dudul Dorjé (1733-1797)	9. Péma Nyinjé Wongpo (1774-1853)
14. Tegchok Dorjé (1798-1868)	10. Péma Kunzang (1854-1885)
15. Kakyab Dorjé (1871-1922)	11. Péma Wongchuk Gyalpo (1886-1952)
16. Rikpé Dorjé (1923-1981)	12. Péma Donyö Nyinjé (1954-)
17. Trinlé Dorjé (1985-)	

Notes

THE ENTHRONEMENT OF A REINCARNATE MASTER

1. *The History of the Kagyu Lineage*, Yama Dorjé et al. (Ganzé, 1989).

2. These are most often presented as three — supreme, ordinary being, and created objects.

3. Two happy exceptions to this rule are found in Chadral Rinpoché and Tai Situ Rinpoché, who have seen fit to create worthy institutions for Himalayan women to learn Buddhism and meditation.

4. This was the Jamgon Kongtrul Rinpoché who died in 1992.

5. Bokar Rinpoché said that Kalu Rinpoché asked for assistance to sit up once again. This was given, over the objections of the doctor. Rinpoché placed his hands in meditation posture and breathed his last.

THE CELEBRATION OF ONE HUNDRED DOORS OF GREAT WONDER

Chapter One: The Five Magnificent Aspects of the Spiritual Master's Manifestation in the World

1. Here Kongtrul identifies Karmapa as an emanation of the bodhisattva Lotus-in-Hand; later, he mentions him to be the bodhisattva All-Seeing

One and, later still, Lord of the World. In fact, these three names indicate the same bodhisattva.

2. The five certainties are characteristics of the body of the perfect splendor of enlightenment: the place (Highest Pure Land); the time (until the end of cyclic existence); the body (marked by every mark and sign of perfection); the speech (instructions of the Great Way); and entourage (high bodhisattvas).

3. "Life of freedom" (Tibetan: *rnam thar*) refers, in this case, to the entire range of activity and experience of an enlightened master. The term is more commonly used to refer to the biographical or autobiographical record of a spiritual master's life.

4. Tibet's reincarnate masters are still commonly called "Living Buddha" (Tibetan: *sangs rgyas dngos*; Mandarin: *ho fo*) by most Chinese persons, including officials of the present government of mainland China, inheritors of the mandate of heaven (Tibetan: *gnam skos*).

5. The listeners and solitary sages are highly developed disciples of the Buddha who have no inclination toward the bodhisattva's ideal of spiritual development for others' sakes.

6. This refers to the fact, mentioned above in the Preface, that Karmapa was the first Tibetan reincarnate master to receive formal recognition.

7. The three regions are above, on, and below the earth.

8. Vajra Chitta (Vajra Mind) and Devi Kotra (Palace of the Goddess) are two names given to the same location. This sacred site is commonly called Tsadra Rinchen Drak (Jewel Cliff, Like Charitra), the name of the cliff which separates the area from Palpung Monastery and an allusion to a major pilgrimage area in south-central Tibet, Charitra.

9. "Dakas and dakinis" in this context refers to male and female enlightened beings who live in three locations — below, on, or above the earth.

10. A *gényen* god is a worldly, local deity who has received Buddhist lay ordination from the spiritual master, who extracted from the deity promises of noninterference with or aid to spiritual practice in their domain.

11. These ten virtues of a region have nothing to do with Buddhist ethical conduct: "The virtues of the land are land for homes and land for cultivation. The virtues of wood are wood for construction and wood for fuel. The virtues of stone are stone for construction and stone for grinding. The virtues of water are water for drinking and water for irrigation. The virtues of grass are close pastures and distant pastures." (Unattributed

quotation cited by Kongtrul in his *Guide to Tsadra Rinchen Drak, Collected Works*, volume 11, pages 477-546. This quotation is found on page 495.)

12. The context of the use of the terms "three worlds" and "three existences" seems poetic rather than literal. Kongtrul does not provide any information on which definition he has in mind: the existences above, on, or below the earth; the existence of desire, form, and formlessness; or the existence of gods, nagas, and human beings.

13. The sun: seven horses pull the chariot on which the god of the sun rides.

14. Some great individuals take multiple rebirths, each of which might be designated as embodying the qualities of the body, speech, mind, talents, or activity of the former master. Thus Chökyi Wongchuk is identified here as the incarnation of the qualities of the speech of Trisong Dé-u Tsen, the king of Tibet who invited Guru Rinpoché to that country in the eighth century.

15. The four means of gathering disciples are generosity, pleasant speech, meaningful acts, and behavior consistent with one's teaching.

16. The eight worldly concerns are joy in gain, sadness in loss, joy in fame, sadness in obscurity, joy in comfort, sadness in discomfort, joy in praise, and sadness in blame.

17. The words "it is translated" in Tibetan are modified by the term "tang log" (*thang log*), presumably a method or style of translation, but not one I have been able to discover the meaning of. "Nine" is clearly written in the text; however, Kongtrul cites ten meanings of the word below and elsewhere (e.g., *Encyclopedia of Buddhism* volume 1, page 334).

18. For Kongtrul's audience, this list would evoke the same immediate recognition as names of groups of musicians would for us. The six ornaments: Nagarjuna, Asanga, Dignaga (the three who composed the basic texts); Aryadeva, Vasubandhu, and Dharmakirti (the three writers of commentaries). The two exemplary masters: Shantideva and Chandragomin. The four great masters: Ashvagosha, Rahulabhadra, Gunaprabha, and Dharmapala. The six gateways to erudition defended the gates of the tantric monastic college of Vikramashila (north-central India) from ideological challenges by non-Buddhist scholars: Ratnashantipa (east gate), Prajnakara (south), Vagisvarakirti (west), Naropa (north), Brahmin Ratnavajra (central, first great pillar), and Jnana Shrimitra (central, second great pillar). (See Kongtrul, *Encyclopedia of Buddhism* volume 1, pages 413, 426).

These masters were all Indian; the following are persons who were involved in the inception of Buddhism in Tibet; all were Tibetans, except for Guru Rinpoché, Atisha, and Dampa Sangyé.

Kongtrul gives this list of the ten main pillars of the scholastic tradition (which differs from that of some other historians):

> In the beginning, the emanation of [the bodhisattva] Gentle Melody, *Thonmi Sambhota*, created the rules of letters and grammar. Then the manifestation of enlightenment, the great translator *Vairochana; Kawa Paltsek; Chokro Lu'i Gyaltsen*; and the noble one of Shang Nanam, *Yeshé Dé*, translated all the instructions of the discourses and tantras, and thus gave the usage of the new language its definitive form. The great Noob, the precious master *Sangyé Yeshé*, widely spread the scholastic tradition, such as those of [the basic Buddhist sources] the discourses and *The Net of Illusion [Tantra]*. The great translator *Rinchen Zangpo* was the first of the later spread [of Buddhism in Tibet]. He and the later Ngok translator *Loden Sherab* translated an infinite number of wisdom mother tantras and treatises of philosophical commentary and initiated the scholastic tradition of most of them. These and the entire range of scholastic traditions from other sources were upheld by the noble *Sakya Ku-ön [Pandita]*, and the precious master *Bu-ton*. These individuals are collectively known by the name "the ten main pillars," upon which the scholastic tradition was raised. Like the sun, they were able to illuminate this dark region, the northern land of Tibet, with the Buddha's teaching. The kindness of these individuals who thus performed the enlightened activity of the Mighty Sage [the Buddha] exceeds the bounds of space. (*Encyclopedia of Buddhism* 1: 504)

According to Kongtrul in *The Ritual of Offering to the Spiritual Masters of the Eight Great Practice Lineages* (*The Treasury of Precious Instructions of Tibetan Buddhism*, volume 16, pages 1-65), the eight originators of the practice lineages of Tibet are Guru Rinpoché, Atisha, Sakya Kunga Nyingpo, Marpa, Kyungpo Naljor, Dampa Sangyé, Tukjé Tsondru, and Orgyenpa. Lists by other scholars may vary.

19. Perhaps it bears repeating that Kongtrul's audience was well aware that Tai Situpa is considered an emanation of this bodhisattva Loving-Kindness (Maitreya).

Chapter Two: Tai Situpa's Special Qualities

1. A universal monarch is literally a "wheel monarch," ruler of all or part of a world: his symbol of authority is a wheel which appears from the sky to signal his ascendency.

2. The age of perfection is a golden age during which human beings do not commit negative acts: among the effects of such virtue are extreme longevity and well-being.

3. The period of the duration of this universe is called the Fortunate Aeon because one thousand buddhas will appear in the world during this time. Shakyamuni Buddha is considered to be the fourth Buddha; thousands of years in the future, the bodhisattva Loving-Kindness will become the fifth.

4. Buddhist writers of almost every day and age have managed to discern the five signs of degeneration filling their worlds: degeneration of longevity, emotions, beings, time, and outlook.

5. The word "appears" is used in the present tense since this bodhisattva and the next one mentioned are considered to be alive and well and living in the Buddha's pure lands at the same time as their emanations live and die in this and other worlds.

6. The pure stages of awakening are the final three — the eighth, ninth, and tenth.

7. The treasure texts written by Guru Rinpoché and concealed by him and his circle of disciples were written on yellow parchment.

8. Charitra (pronounced *Tsaritra* in Tibetan), an area of sacred ground in south-central Tibet, has been very important to lamas of the Kagyu tradition. It ("old" Charitra) was first inaugurated by a disciple of Gampopa and was later renewed by this former life of Tai Situpa, who was also known as Yeshé Wongchuk.

9. Perhaps this emperor was considered a miracle worker since his guests from India (the sixteen elders and Virupa) had, by all accounts, been dead for hundreds of years. With only the name or title "Tashing" to go by, it is difficult to identify this person with certainty; however, since his contemporary mentioned here, the fourth Karmapa, Rolpé Dorjé, spent four years (1359-63) at the court of the last emperor of the Yuan Dynasty, that emperor is quite likely the one Kongtrul refers to as Tashing. *The Cambridge History of China* offers a somewhat less flattering report than Kongtrul would of this emperor, Toghon Temur (1320-70; reigned 1333-68):

> By all the signs, Toghon Temur, now thirty-four years of age, had withdrawn into a kind of semiretirement. He was regularly participating with a select circle of adepts, and an all-female dance ensemble and orchestra, in the sexual rituals of Tibetan Buddhism. On at least one occasion, he sponsored a holy circumambulation of the imperial palace grounds by a group of 108 monks. He was also having built a huge pleasure boat (the model for it was of his

own making) for sailing on the lake in the imperial palace, and he himself also had a major hand in the design and fashioning of a large, technically elaborate clepsydra, or water clock. Perhaps in order to accommodate the new boat, a costly project was later undertaken to dredge the palace waterways. (volume 6, page 579)

Perhaps it should be noted that the Yuan Dynasty emperors, such as Toghon Temur, were Mongol, not Han Chinese.

10. Again, although this text does not name the emperor, it is likely Yung-lo (reigned 1403-1424), the emperor who offered the black crown to Déshin Shekpa, the fifth Karmapa. (See Appendix). *The Cambridge History of China* provides this picture of the relationship between the Chinese political (Yung-lo, 1360-1424) and the Tibetan spiritual (Déshin Shekpa) emperors:

> De-bzin-gsegs-pa (known to the Chinese as Halima, 1384-1415) was famous as a miracle worker, and his reputation had reached the Yung-lo emperor while he was still Prince of Yen. After his accession to the throne in 1403, the new emperor sent a mission to Tibet. The mission invited De-bzin-gsegs-pa to Nanking. After first sending a tribute mission, De-bzin-gsegs-pa came in person to the Ming court in April 1407 and was lavishly received. Asked to perform religious ceremonies on behalf of the emperor's deceased parents, it is recorded that he performed many miraculous feats, producing visions of various deities, apparitions of cranes and lions, flowers falling from the sky, sweet dew, and so forth for twenty-two days. Richly rewarded, he and members of his retinue were granted resounding official titles. (volume 7, pages 262-63)

Karmapa was given the title "Transcendent One, precious spiritual king, the western great Loving-Kindness; Buddha, lord of peace." ("Transcendent One" is a translation of the meaning of his name in Tibetan; he is called "western" since Tibet — "the western treasure-house" in Chinese — lies to the west of China.) To this day, he is known to the Chinese by part of this title, "precious spiritual king" (*Da-bao Fa-wong* in Mandarin). Karmapa did not adopt this title in Tibet, as he had already been known there as Karmapa for two centuries prior to this event. One of the Chinese titles Chökyi Gyaltsen received at that time from the emperor, Tai Situ, stayed with his incarnations, as this marked the first of his line.

11. Tai Situpa's formal name is usually abbreviated to Kenting Tai Situpa — Kenting is a Tibetan transliteration of Chinese perhaps faithful to the pronunciation of another era. In modern Mandarin, *kuan-ting*, as Kongtrul has written and translated it into Tibetan (*spyi bo nas dbang bskur*), is the

word commonly used for *empowerment. Tai,* now pronounced *Da* in Mandarin, means "great"; *Situ* is a Chinese title; *pa* is a Tibetan suffix indicating, in this case, the holder of the title.

12. Kongtrul refers to Tai Situpa's crown sometimes as "a red crown radiant with gold," sometimes as "a dark-red crown" or "a red crown." For more details of this important trademark of the Tai Situpa, see the Appendix.

13. The four means of liberation are the ways an ordinary individual makes an initial connection to a bodhisattva or buddha so that the seed of liberation is planted — through seeing, hearing, remembering, and being touched by the bodhisattva or buddha.

14. The three realms are those of desire, the gods of form, and the gods of formlessness.

15. This passage is taken from a treasure text; therefore, the author is presumably Guru Rinpoché. Samantabhadra, a Sanskrit name written in the Tibetan text, corresponds to Kunzang in Tibetan, thus pointing to Péma Kunzang.

16. According to some predictions, Buddhism deteriorates during ten five-hundred-year periods, starting from the time of the Buddha. Despite the fact that barely 2,500 years have now elapsed since the Buddha's death, writers have claimed for centuries that they and their readers live in the last of the five-hundred-year periods, when all that remains of Buddhism is a mere outward semblance of spiritual practice.

Chapter Three: A Step-by-Step Description of Enthronement and the Presentation of Offerings

1. The ten forces are forces gained through knowledge of right and wrong; the maturation of acts; meditation, liberation, absorption, and concentration, etc.; the various levels of capability of beings; the various inclinations of others; various worlds; the paths which lead to higher existences and liberation; his own former lives; the past and future birthplaces and deaths of others; and the dissipation of all obscurations. The four forms of confidence (literally, "fearlessness") are confidence regarding attainment of awakening, the dissipation of impurities, teaching concerning obstacles to the spiritual path, and teaching of the certain path to liberation. The four bases of miracles are will, diligence, mind, and analysis. The ten powers are power of longevity, mind, possessions, activity, inclination,

rebirth, aspiration, miracles, wisdom, and spiritual instruction. The four forms of enlightened activity are pacifying, enhancing, magnetizing, and overpowering.

2. The two extremes are the beliefs in nihilism and permanence.

3. The three-thousand-realmed universe is a galaxy consisting of this world-system, multiplied by a thousand; this in turn is multiplied a thousand times; and this thousand times a thousand is again multiplied a thousand times.

4. Kongtrul is likely referring to the eight subjects of the text, mentioned in its prologue:

> The perfection of wisdom is taught in eight subjects: (1) knowledge of all forms; (2) knowledge of the path; this is followed by (3) knowledge of everything; (4) complete realization of all forms; (5) reaching the summit; (6) culmination; (7) instantaneous manifest, complete awakening; and (8) the ultimate body of enlightenment. (*The Ornament of Realization*, in *Byams chos sde lnga*; Beijing, 1993; page 2)

5. The eight auspicious substances are a mirror, yogurt, *durva* grass, *bilba* fruit, a conch shell which turns clockwise, medicine from elephant brain, vermilion powder, and white mustard seed. The eight auspicious symbols are a knot, a lotus, a parasol, a conch shell, a wheel, a victory banner, a vase, and a pair of golden fishes. The seven precious articles of the monarch are described in the text below. All these offerings are presented to the recipient in the form of drawings.

6. Offerings to the monastic community have always been considered one of the main ways for a devoted Buddhist to cultivate merit.

7. Mandalas used as a support for meditation are not described in this text. For Kongtrul's explanation of their use, see Jamgon Kongtrul, *The Torch of Certainty*, translated by Judith Hanson (Boulder: Shambhala, 1977), Chapter 4.

8. "Water of cow excretions" is a reminder that Buddhism was born and bred in India: the many excretions of a cow were considered particularly auspicious. An extremely distilled, concentrated form would be used for this occasion.

9. Huge discs of the elements support the foundation of this world: for Kongtrul's description of the worlds of Buddhist cosmology, see *Myriad Worlds*, translated by the International Translation Committee (Ithaca: Snow Lion, 1995).

10. A *yojana* is the basic measure used for large distances in Buddhist texts. One *yojana* equals 16,000 cubits. If a cubit is estimated to be 18 inches, a *yojana* equals 4.54 miles. The word has been preserved in translation in order that the same numbers be used.

11. I find this sentence objectionable and disheartening, particularly from the pen of Kongtrul. Although I have considered deleting it altogether from the translation, it remains, to serve as an example of Buddhist scholarship at its worst and as a warning that such words could be written unthinkingly even by an otherwise enlightened master.

12. The seven semiprecious articles also belong to a monarch. Each has extraordinary qualities: a fine precious palace, a bed, boots, a sword, clothing, a snake skin, and a grove.

13. According to Tulku Thubten, the *rtsa* (root, source, or base) in the text should be read as *rtse* (peak, summit, or highest point).

14. The three trainings are in ethics, meditation, and wisdom. Although the original text reads "two" cycles, this is probably an error for the three cycles — of study and reflection, meditation, and activity.

15. The four kinds of magnificence refers to material and worldly splendor in four domains — spiritual instruction, wealth, comfort, and freedom.

16. The Karma Kamtsang is another name for the Karma Kagyu, the monastic system headed by Karmapa.

Appendix: Spiritual Kings and Crowns

1. *Mngon mtong* in the text is read here as *mngon mtho*, "uplifting," a reference to the paths of worldly religions which ensure their followers freedom from rebirth in miserable, lower realms and happy future lives in the heavens or on earth. "Certain satisfaction" refers to the results of the Buddhist paths: freedom and enlightenment.

2. The three kings referred to are Song-tsen Gampo, Trisong Dé-u Tsen, and Tri-tsuk Dé-tsen, this last also known by a nickname, Tri Ralpa-chen.

3. Jowo Shakyamuni is the name of the statue of the Buddha that has given its name to the temple which houses it, the central temple of Lhasa, the Jo-khang.

4. For more information on Yung-lo, see note 10 to Chapter Two.

5. The fifth Garwong refers to the fifth Shamar Rinpoché, known by two names, Konchok Bong and Konchok Yenlak (1525-1583). Later he refers

to the Shamars as Gargyi Wongpo, an elaboration of Garwong. He does not use the title "Shamar" in this text except when referring to all the red crowns worn by Tai Situpa, Gyaltsab, and Shamarpa.

6. The three ways to please the spiritual master are to make offerings, to serve him or her, and to put the instructions one has received into practice.

7. The four means of liberation are the ways a connection to a bodhisattva can be made so that the seed of liberation is planted — through sight, hearing, remembering, and touch.

8. In his autobiography, Kongtrul mentions that he requested and easily received custody of Payma Kunzang from the monastic administration of Tashi Lhunpo, not that of Sera.

9. This journey would take a proficient rider on a good horse the better part of a day of hard riding.

10. The term used here is *si* (pronounced *see*; written *sri*), considered to be reincarnated very harmful spirits of those who have broken tantric commitments.

11. Kongtrul does nothing to explain this astounding oversight: normally, the death of any head of a large monastery, and certainly that of a leader of Tai Situpa's stature, would be accompanied by ceremonies lasting forty-nine days. As Kongtrul mentions, in the case of a high spiritual master or reincarnate master, this period is not one of mourning but of thanksgiving offerings to the master on the part of his or her disciples.

Names Mentioned in the Text

Aniruddha (Unobstructed) was one of the ten close Listener disciples of the Buddha, the foremost among them in higher perception (literally, eyes of the gods). Mentioned as having been a former life of one reincarnate lama of Tai Situpa's entourage.

Ashvaghosha (probably 1st century CE) was an Indian scholar who wrote a collection of the former lives of the Buddha.

Atisha (982-1054) was the Indian meditation master and scholar whose arrival in Tibet marked the beginning of the later phase of religious exchange between India and Tibet.

Buddhaguhya (Buddha Secret) (8th century) was among the Indian pandits invited to Tibet by King Trisong De-u Tsen to spread tantric Buddhism in his country.

Chandrakirti (Moon of Renown) (c. 600-650) was a great Indian scholar mentioned in this text as the author of *Entering the Middle Way.*

Chödrak Gyatso (*Chos grag rgya mtsho*; Ocean of Renown in Spiritual Instruction) (1454-1506) was the seventh Karmapa.

Chökyi Gocha (*Chos kyi go cha*; Armor of the Doctrine) (1542-85) was the fourth Tai Situpa.

Chökyi Gyaltsen (*Chos kyi rgyal mtshan*; Victory Banner of Spiritual Instruction) (1377-1448) was the first Tai Situpa.

Chökyi Gyaltsen Gélek Palzangpo (*Chos kyi rgyal mtshan dGe legs dpal bzang po*; Victory Banner of Spiritual Instruction; Glorious and Excellent Virtue) (1586-1657), the fifth Tai Situpa, received the red crown from the ninth Karmapa.

Chökyi Jungné (*Chos kyi 'byung gnas*: Source of Spiritual Instruction) (1700-1774) was the eighth, and by all accounts, greatest Tai Situpa.

Chökyi Wongchuk (*Chos kyi dbang phyug*; Master of Spiritual Instruction) (1212-1270), usually called Guru Chöwong, was one of the early great treasure revealers.

Chögyal Mipam Trinlé Rabten (*Chos rgyal Mi pham phrin las rab brtan*; King of Spiritual Instructions, Invincible Completely Firm Activity) (1658-1682) was the sixth Tai Situpa.

Chöying Dorjé (*Chos dbying rdo rje*; Vajra of the Sphere of Totality) (1604-1674) was the tenth Karmapa.

Da-ö Shunnu (*Zla ba gzhon nu*; Youthful Moon) or **Dawkpo Da-ö Shunnu** (*Dvags po* is a place name) (*see* Gampopa)

Dawkpo Go-nyon (*Dvags po sGo smyon*) was a former life of Dondrup Tulku, the close attendant of the eighth Karmapa, thus probably 16th century.

Darikapa, a past life of Tai Situpa, was one of the eighty-four great accomplished tantric masters of Buddhist India.

Denma Tsémang (*lDan ma rtse mang*) (8th century), a past life of Tai Situpa, was a translator — one of the three senior translators — and meditation master at the time of Guru Rinpoché's sojourn in Tibet.

Déshek Pagmo Drupa (*De gshegs Pag mo gru pa*; Transcendent One) (1110-1170), a disciple of Gampopa, founded the Padru Kagyu system, one of the four great Kagyu monastic systems; his disciples founded the eight lesser Kagyu monastic schools.

Déshin Shekpa (*De bzhin gshegs pa*; Transcendent One) (1384-1415) was the fifth Karmapa.

Dombipa, a past life of Tai Situpa, was one of the eighty-four great accomplished tantric masters of Indian Buddhism.

Drogon Réchen Sonam Drakpa (*'Gro mgon Ras chen bSod nams grags pa*; Protector of Beings, Great Cotton-Clad One, Renowned Merit) (1148-1218), a past life of Tai Situpa, was the main disciple of the first Karmapa.

Dudul Dorjé (*bDud 'dul rdo rje*; Demon-Conquering Vajra) (1733-1797) was the thirteenth Karmapa.

Dusum Kyenpa (*Dus gsum mkhyen pa*; Knower of the Three Times) (1110-1193) was the first Karmapa.

Ga the Translator (*rGa lo*) no information found.

Gampopa (*sGam po pa*) (1079-1153) was the foremost disciple of Milarepa and the master to the first Karmapa.

Garwong (contraction for **Gargyi Wongpo**, *Gar gyi dbang po*; Lord of the Dance) refers, in this text, to any of the Shamar Rinpochés. The one cited, the fifth, is **Kon-chok Yenlak** (*dKon mchog yan lag*; Jewel Tributary) (1525-1583).

Gompo Tsultrim Nyingpo (*Gom po Tshul khrims snying po*; Heart of Ethics), a past life of Tai Situpa, is mentioned as having been the main recipient of the Great Seal meditation transmission from Gampopa. Probably twelfth century.

Guna Sanskrit for "qualities"; *Yon tan* in Tibetan. This is how Kongtrul signed his text on the red crown. *See* Karma Ngawang Yonten Gyatso.

Guna Nata *See* Yutok Yonten Gonpo.

Guru Rinpoché (8th century) is the Indian master responsible for the implantation of tantric Buddhism throughout the Himalayan region and his presence continues to permeate spiritual life there.

Gyim Shang *See* Jampal Sangwa.

Humkara (8th century) was an Indian meditation master who was one of the main contributors to what became known in Tibet as the Ancient (Nyingma) Instruction Lineage.

Jamgon Kongtrul (*'Jam mgon Kong sprul*; Gentle Protector, Kongpo Vamteng Tulku) (1813-1899), was one of the foremost meditation masters and writers of nineteenth-century Tibet.

Jampal Drakpa (*'Jam dpal grags pa*; Gentle Splendor, Renown) is mentioned as a master who wrote one version of mandala offerings. Mentioned in this text with a Tibetan name but is likely an Indian, possibly Manjushri-kirti.

Jampal Sangwa (*'Jam dpal gsang ba*; Gentle Melody, Secret) (8th century), a past life of Tai Situpa, was a Chinese master of geomancy who analyzed the proposed site for Tibet's first monastery at Samyé.

Jamyang Kyentsé Wongpo (*'Jam dbyangs mKhyen brtse dbang po*; Gentle Melody, Power of Wisdom and Love) (1820-1892), like his disciple and friend, Jamgon Kongtrul, Kyentsé was one of the foremost meditation masters and writers of nineteenth-century Tibet.

Jangchub Dorjé (*Byang chub rdo rje*; Vajra of Awakening) (1703-1732) was the twelfth Karmapa.

Jétari is an Indian master credited with a version of the mandala offering. Dates unavailable.

Jikten Sumgon (*'Jig rten gsum mgon*; Protector of the Three Worlds) (1143-1217) founded the Drigung Kagyu monastic system.

Jivadhyana (*see* Kumarajiva)

Kakyab Dorjé (*mKha' khyab rdo rje*) (1871-1922) was the fifteenth Karmapa, one of the main disciples of Jamgon Kongtrul.

Kambala is an Indian master mentioned in this text as an author of one version of mandala offerings. Dates unavailable.

Karma Drubgyu Tenzin Trinlé Chok (*Karma sGrub brgyud bsTan 'dzin phrin las mchog*; Holder of the Practice Lineage, Supreme Enlightened Activity) was the name of the nineteenth-century reincarnation of one of the Öntrul Rinpochés.

Karma Ngawang Yonten Gyatso (*Karma Ngag dbang yon taṇ rgya mtsho*; Eloquent Ocean of Qualities) is the name Kongtrul uses to sign his book. (*see* Jamgon Kongtrul)

Karma Pakshi (*Karma pakshi*) (1204-1283) was the second Karmapa.

Karma Sidral (*Karma Srid bral*; Free from Ordinary Existence) (*see* Dawkpo Go-nyon)

Karma Tegchok Tenpel (*Karma Theg mchog bsTan 'phel*; He Who Spreads the Doctrine of the Supreme Way) was the name of the nineteenth-century incarnation of one of the Öntrul Rinpochés.

Katok Dampa Déshek (*Ka thok dam pa De shegs*; Holy Transcendent One of Katok) (1122-1192) founded Katok Monastery, one of the largest Nyingma monasteries in eastern Tibet, in 1159. He was the younger brother of Pagmo Drupa.

King Prasenajit was a disciple of the Buddha mentioned in this text as the one who requested the Buddha to perform miracles.

Köntön Lu-i Wongpo (*Khon ston Klu'i dbang po*; Khon Clan Teacher, Master of Nagas) (8th century) was one of three middle translators at the time of Guru Rinpoché.

Kumarajiva (or Jivadhyana) was a disciple of the Buddha who served as physician to King Bimbisara.

Langdro Translator, Konchok Jungné (*dKon mchog 'Byung gnas*; Source of the Rare and Sublime) (8th century) was one of the twenty-five main disciples of Guru Rinpoché.

Lekshé Mawé Nyima (*Legs gshad sMra'i nyi ma*; Sun of Appropriate Verbal Expression) (1683-1698) was the seventh Tai Situpa.

Lo Répa (*Lo Ras pa*; Cotton-Clad Yogi) (1185-1250) was a great meditator of the Drukpa Kagyu tradition. His complete name is Lo Répa Wongchuk Tsondru (*dBang phyug rtson 'grus*; Powerful Diligence).

Longsal Nyingpo (*kLong gsal snying po*; Essence of the Clear Expanse) (1685-1752) was a great treasure revealer.

Lotus-Born (*see* Guru Rinpoché)

Loving-Kindness (Skt. Maitreya; Tib. Jampa; *Byams pa*) was one of the eight great bodhisattva-disciples of the Buddha and the one designated by the Buddha as his regent.

Machik Labdron (*Ma gcig Lab sgron*; Unique Mother, Lamp from Lab) (1031-1129), one of the greatest Tibetan meditation masters, founded the Severance Instruction (Chöd) Lineage.

Marpa the Translator (1012-1097), a past life of Tai Situpa, was the father of the Oral Instruction (Kagyu) lineage in Tibet.

Matiratna (Intellect Jewel) was a great Indian tantric meditation master, mentioned in this text as a former life of Karmapa. Dates unavailable.

Métripa was a great meditation master of eleventh-century India, the principal teacher of Great Seal meditation to the Tibetan master Marpa.

Mikyö Dorjé (*Mi bskyod rdo rje*; Unmoving Vajra) (1507-1554) was the eighth Karmapa.

Milarepa (*Mi la ras pa*) (1040-1123) was Tibet's great yogi-poet, disciple of Marpa and master to Gampopa.

Mingyur Dorjé Drakpo Nuden Tsal (*Mi 'gyur rdo rje Drag po nus ldan rtsal*; Eternal Vajra of Forceful Power) (1688?-?) was a great treasure revealer.

Mitruk Chökyi Özer Go-cha (*Mi khrugs chos kyi 'od zer go cha*; Unperturbed Radiant Spiritual Instructions, Armor) (1542-1585) was the fourth Tai Situpa.

Mutri Tsenpo (*Mu khri tshan po*) (8th century), one of the sons of King Trisong Dé-u Tsen, was a close disciple of Guru Rinpoché.

Nagarjuna was one of the foremost scholars and meditation masters of Buddhist India.

Naropa was a great meditation master of eleventh-century India, the principal teacher of the Tibetan master Marpa.

Ngawang Jikten Wongchuk (*Ngag dbang 'jig rten dbang phyug*; Eloquent Master of the World), a past life of Tai Situpa, is mentioned as having been a king of Rin-poong. Dates unavailable.

Niguma, a great Indian meditation master of the eleventh century, provided the meditation instructions which form the core of the Shangpa Instruction Lineage of Tibet.

Norbu Sampel (*Nor bu bsam phel*; Wish-Granting Gem) (dates not available) is mentioned as one of the previous reincarnations of Öntrul Rinpoché.

Nyokmé Dorjé (*rNyogs med rdo rje*; Flawless Vajra) was an Indian master credited with a version of mandala offerings.

Nyokmé Pal (*rNyogs med dpal*; Flawless Glory) was an Indian master credited with a version of mandala offerings.

Öntrul Rinpoché (*dBon sprul Rin po che*) was a title given to two reincarnate masters close to the ninth Tai Situpa.

Orgyen Chok-gyur Déchen Lingpa (*O rgyan mChog gyur bDe chen gling pa*; Oddiyana, Supreme Great Bliss Island) (1829-1870). This master, disciple, and friend of Kongtrul was a great treasure revealer.

Orgyenpa (1230-1309) was the Tibetan master who first recognized a Tibetan child as a reincarnate master (the third Karmapa, Rangjung Dorjé).

Padmakara (Lotus-Born) (*see* Guru Rinpoché)

Padmasambhava (Lotus-Born) (*see* Guru Rinpoché)

Pakpa Rinpoché (also known as Pakpa Lodru Gyaltsen ('*Phags pa Blo gros rgyal mtshan*; Exalted Victory Banner of the Intellect) (1235-1280), nephew of Sakya Pandita, was one of the five founding fathers of the Sakya monastic tradition.

Pang Kenchen Özer Lama, a past life of Tai Situpa, was a Tibetan master, perhaps of the Kadampa tradition since he appears in the lineage of mind training two names from Chékawa, author of *The Seven Points of Mind Training*. Dates unavailable.

Péma Donyö Nyinjé (*Padma Don yod nyin byed*; Lotus, Meaningful Sun) (b. 1954) is the present Tai Situpa, the twelfth.

Péma Kunzang (*Padma Kun bzang*; Lotus, Ever-Excellent) (1854-1885) (also known as Péma Kunzang Chökyi Gyalpo; *Chos kyi rgyal po*; King of Spiritual Instructions) was the tenth Tai Situpa, for whose enthronement Kongtrul wrote this text.

Péma Nyinjé Wongpo (*Pad ma Nyin byed dbang po*; Lotus, Powerful Sun) (1774-1853), the ninth Tai Situpa, was the principal spiritual master of Jamgon Kongtrul.

Péma Wongchuk Gyalpo (*Pad ma dBang phyug rgyal po*; Lotus, Powerful Lord, King) (1886-1952) was the eleventh Tai Situpa, the master of many modern Kagyu teachers, including the sixteenth Karmapa and Kalu Rinpoché.

Rabten Kunzang Pak (*Rab rtan Kun bzang 'phags*; Stable Ever-Excellent, Exalted), a past life of Tai Situpa, is mentioned in this text as having been king of Gyantsé, a city in west-central Tibet. Dates unavailable.

Rangjung Dorjé (*Rang byung rdo rje*; Self-Arisen Vajra) (1284-1339) was the third Karmapa and the first reincarnate master recognized in Tibet.

Ratna Bhadra from **Ringo** (Ringo is a Tibetan place name; Ratna Bhadra is Sanskrit for Excellent Jewel) (14th century), a past life of Tai Situpa, was the chief disciple of the third Karmapa.

Ratna Lingpa (Jewel Island) (1403-1479) was a great treasure revealer.

Réchungpa (*Ras chung pa*) (1083-1161) was one of the closest disciples of Milarepa.

Rikpé Dorjé (*Rig pa'i rdo rje*; Vajra of Awareness) (1923-81) was the sixteenth Karmapa, who travelled widely in the West.

Rinchen Puntsok (*Rin chen phun tshogs*; Magnificent Jewel) (1449-1497) was a great master of the Drigung Kagyu monastic system.

Rolpé Dorjé (*Rol pa'i rdo rje*; Playful Vajra) (1340-1383) was the fourth Karmapa.

Rolpé Dorjé Ta-dun Trin-dra Tayé Tsal (*Rol pa'i rdo rje rTa bdun sprin 'dra mtha' yas rtsal*; Playful Vajra, Sun, Infinite Like Clouds Adept) (17th century) was a treasure revealer.

Sangyé Lama (*Sangs gyas bla ma*; Buddha Spiritual Master) (1000-1080) was the first Tibetan discoverer of treasure texts.

Saraha was a great tantric meditation master of India. He is mentioned in this text as a former life of Karmapa.

Shakyamuni Buddha (Sage of the Shakyas) was the historical Buddha.

Shantideva (God of Peace) was an accomplished meditation master of Indian tantric Buddhism who wrote some key works concerning the training of the bodhisattva.

Shri Singha (Illustrious Lion), a past life of Tai Situpa, was a Chinese meditation master who taught Great Completion (Dzok Chen) meditation to Guru Rinpoché.

Source of Spiritual Instructions (Tib. Chökyi Jungné; *Chos kyi 'byung gnas*): The name of one of Tai Situpa's emanations, a bodhisattva who lives in the pure land Blissful. Not to be confused with the eighth Tai Situpa of the same name.

Sucharita, an Indian master, was mentioned in this text as an author of one version of mandala offerings.

Sukasiddhi (Accomplishment of Bliss) (11th century), a great Indian meditation master, provided the meditation instructions which form part of the Shangpa Instruction Lineage of Tibet.

Tang-tong Gyalpo (*Thang stong rgyal po*; King of the Plain of Emptiness) (1385-1464) was a great meditation master who figures in a number of Tibetan lineages of tantric meditation.

Taranata (*Taranatha*; Protector of Liberation) (1575-1635), a past life of Tai Situpa, was a great meditation master of the Vajra Yoga and Shangpa Instruction Lineages.

Tashi Namgyal (*bKra shis rnam rgyal*; Auspicious Total Victor) (1450-1497) was the second Tai Situpa.

Tashi Özer (*bKra shis 'od zer*; Auspicious Radiance) (19th century) was one of the main disciples of Jamgon Kongtrul.

Tashing (14th century), a past life of Tai Situpa, was emperor of China and is mentioned in this book as having had miraculous powers. Possibly Toghon Temur (1320-1370), the last emperor of the Yuan Dynasty.

Tashi Paljor (*bKra shis dpal 'byor*; Auspicious Glory and Wealth) (1499-1541) was the third Tai Situpa.

Tegchok Dorjé (*Theg mchog rdo rje*; Vajra of the Supreme Way) (1798-1868), the fourteenth Karmapa, recognized the tenth Tai Situpa and attended his enthronement.

Tenpa Nyinjé (*bsTan pa nyin byed*; Sun of the Doctrine) (*see* Chökyi Jungné)

Toghon Temur (*see* Tashing)

Tongwa Donden (*mThong ba don ldan*; Meaningful to Behold) (1416-1453) was the sixth Karmapa.

Trinlé Dorjé (*Phrin las rdo rje*; Vajra of Enlightened Activity) (b.1985) is the present Karmapa, the seventeenth.

Tsangpa Lha'i Métok (*Tshangs pa lha'i me tok*; Flower of the Gods of Brahma) (8th century) is better known as King Trisong Dé-u Tsen, the Tibetan king who invited Guru Rinpoché to introduce tantric Buddhism in his kingdom.

Vasubandhu was a great scholar of Indian Buddhism.

Virupa (11th century) was one of the great accomplished masters of Indian tantric Buddhism.

Wongchuk Dorjé (*dBang phyug rdo rje*; Powerful Vajra) (1555-1603) was the ninth Karmapa.

White Crown Ornament was the name of the Buddha during his last rebirth before his life as Shakyamuni.

Yeshé Dorjé (*Ye shes rdo rje*; Wisdom Vajra) (1676-1702) was the eleventh Karmapa.

Yeshé Ö (*Ye shes 'od*; Light of Wisdom) (13th century), a past life of Tai Situpa, served as a close attendant to the second Karmapa.

Yeshé Tsogyal (*Ye shes mtsho rgyal*; Queen of the Lake of Wisdom) (8th century) was one of the principal disciples of Guru Rinpoché.

Yung-lo (1360-1424), emperor of China during the Ming Dynasty (reigned 1403-1424), gave the black crown to the fifth Karmapa and probably the title Tai Situ to Chökyi Gyaltsen, the first Tai Situpa.

Yutok Yonten Gonpo (*gYu thog Yon tan mgon po*; Turquoise Roof, Protector of Qualities) (12th century) was a major source of the Tibetan medical tradition.

Texts Cited

TEXTS CITED BY THE TRANSLATOR

The Autobiography of Jamgon Kongtrul (*Phyogs med ris med kyi bstan pa la 'dun shing dge sbyong gi gzugs brnyan 'chang ba blo gros mtha' yas kyi sde'i byung ba brjod pa nor bu sna tshogs mdog can*). *The Collected Works of Jamgon Kongtrul*, volume 16, pages 59-478.

A Brief Introduction on the Occasion of the Presentation of the Precious Red Crown Which Liberates on Sight, Describing the Reasons for and the Benefits of Seeing It (*mThong grol sva dmar rin po che mjal kai skabs rgyu mtshan phan yon mdor bsdus gling pa*). *The Collected Works of Jamgon Kongtrul*, volume 9, pages 311-18.

The Biography of Jamyang Kyentsé Wongpo (*rJe btsun bla ma thams cad mkhyen cing gzigs pa 'jam dbyangs mkhyen brtse'i dbang po kun dga' bstan pa'i rgyal mtshan dpal bzang po'i rnam thar mdor bsdus pa ngo mtshar u dumba ra'i dga' 'tshal*). *The Collected Works of Jamgon Kongtrul*, volume 15.

The Celebration of the Opening of One Hundred Doors to Great Wonder (*Byams mgon mchog gi sprul pa'i sku seng ge'i khrir phebs pa'i mandala rgyas bshad ngo mtshar sgo bryga 'byed pa'i dga' ston*). *The Collected Works of Jamgon Kongtrul*, volume 9, pages 121-77.

The Encyclopedia of Buddhism (*Shes bya kun la khyab pa'i gzhung lugs nyung ngu'i tshig gis rnam par 'grel ba legs bshad yongs 'du shes bya mtha' yas pa'i rgya mtsho*) by Jamgon Kongtrul (Beijing: People's Press, 1985).

The History of the Kagyu Lineage (*bKa' brgyud lo rgyu gsar bsgrigs dbyar gyi rlu gsang*) by Yama Dorjé et al. (Ganzé, 1989).

The Royal Prayer of Aspirations (*Ni gu ma'i smon lam bka' rgya ma*; also known as *'Phags pa smon lam gyi rgyal po*) by Niguma; contained in *The Treasury of Profound Instructions* (one of Kongtrul's Five Treasuries), volume 12, pages 459-62.

TEXTS CITED BY JAMGON KONGTRUL

An Approach to the Ultimate (*Don dam bsnyen pa*) by Pundarika.

The Condensed Version of the Perfection of Wisdom Discourse (*Phar phyin sdud pa*).

The Declarations (*Tshoms*), probably *Ched du brjod pa'i tshoms*.

The Discourse of the Symbol of Moving to Courage on the Heads of All Buddhas (*Sangs rgyas thams cad kyi gtsug tor dpa' bar 'gro ba phyag rgya'i mdo*).

The Discourse Requested by Renowned as Pure (*Dri ma med par grags pas zhus pa'i mdo*).

The Discourse Requested by Sagaramati (*Blo gros rgya mtshos zhus pa'i mdo*).

The Discourse Which Reveals Inconceivable Secrets (*gSang ba bsam gyis mi khyab par bstan pa'i mdo*).

Entering the Middle Way (*dBu ma la 'jug pa*) by Chandrakirti.

Entering the Path to Awakening (*Byang chub sems dpa' spyod pa la 'jug pa*) by Shantideva.

The Extensive Tantra of Great Illusion (*sGyu 'phrul rgyas pa*).

Fifty Verses in Praise of the Spiritual Master (*lNga bcu pa*) by Aryashura.

The Five Stages of the Union of Secrets (*gSang 'dus rim lnga*).

The Flourishing of Great Liberation Discourse (*Thar pa chen po phyogs su rgyas pa'i mdo*).

The Flower Ornament Discourse (*Avatamsaka Sutra*; *Phal po che'i mdo*).

The Former Lives of the Buddha (*sKyes rabs*) Kongtrul does not specify whether this refers to accounts given by the Buddha or to a later text.

The Great Enjoyment Discourse (*rGya chen rol pa'i mdo*).

The Great Prophecy of the Union of the Master's Enlightened Vision (*Bla ma dgongs 'dus kyi lung bstan chen mo*) perhaps a treasure text revealed by Sangyé Lingpa (1340-1396).

The Group of Spiritual Instructions from Yel-Puk at Namka Dzö (*Yel phug nam mkha' mdzod kyi chos sde*) texts discovered by Chokgyur Déchen Lingpa.

The Highest Continuity (*rGyud bla ma*) by the bodhisattva Maitreya.

The Illustrious Gathering (*dPal ldan 'dus pa*) This is perhaps a text on the subject of the deity Gathering of Secrets (Guhyasamaja).

The Jewel Palm Discourse (*dKon mchog ta li'i mdo*)

The Lamp of Jewels Discourse (*dKon mchog sgron me'i mdo*).

The Mandala Discourse (*Mandal gyi mdo*).

The Ornament of Realization (*mNgon rtogs rgyan*) by the bodhisattva Maitreya.

The Ornament of the Discourses (*mDo sde rgyan*) by the bodhisattva Maitreya.

Principles of Elucidation (*rNam bshad rigs pa*) by Vasubandhu.

The Profound Inner Meaning (*Zab mo nang gi don*) by the third Karmapa, Rangjung Dorjé.

The Reunion of Father and Child Discourse (*'Phags pa yab sras mjal ba'i mdo*).

The River of Salt Water Discourse (*Ba tsha can gyi chu klung gi mdo*).

A Section of the Root Tantra of the Wheel of Time (*Dus 'khor rtsa rgyud kyi dum bu*).

The Sovereign Tantra of the General Empowerment of All Joyful Ones within the Vital Essence of Buddha Vairochana (*De bzhin gshegs pa thams cad kyi spyi dbang rnam par snang mdzad thig ler dbang bskur ba rgyal po'i rgyud*).

The Sublime Pinnacle of Jewels Discourse (*'Phags pa dkon mchog brtsegs pa'i mdo*).

The Transmission of Discipline (*'Dul ba lung*) There are four texts in the series of texts on monastic discipline as defined by the Buddha. Kongtrul does not specify which he has quoted.

The Treasury of Knowledge (*mNgon pa mdzod*) by Vasubandhu.

The Two Chapters (*brTag pa gnyis pa*) the tantra of Hevajra.

The Vajra Heart Ornament Tantra (*rDo rje snying po rgyan gyi rgyud*).

RELATED WORKS BY JAMGON KONGTRUL IN ENGLISH

Myriad Worlds, translated by the International Translation Committee (Ithaca: Snow Lion, 1995).

The Torch of Certainty, translated by Judith Hanson (Boulder: Shambhala, 1977). See Chapter Four for a description of the offering of mandalas.